THE CONSUMER FINANCE INDUSTRY
Its Costs and Regulation

THE CONSUMER FINANCE INDUSTRY

Its Costs and Regulation

EDITED BY

JOHN M. CHAPMAN
Professor Emeritus of Banking

ROBERT P. SHAY
Professor of Banking and Finance

A Report of the GRADUATE SCHOOL OF BUSINESS
COLUMBIA UNIVERSITY

Published by COLUMBIA UNIVERSITY PRESS
New York and London
1967

Advisory Committee

JOSEPH H. TAGGART, Chairman
Dean, Graduate School of Business Administration,
New York University

S. LEES BOOTH
Director of Research,
National Consumer Finance Association

DAVID CAPLOVITZ
Associate Professor of Sociology,
Columbia University

ERNST A. DAUER
Director of Consumer Credit Studies,
Household Finance Corporation

FRANK L. FERNBACH
Assistant Director,
AFL-CIO Research Department

J. DEANE GANNON
Director,
Bureau of Federal Credit Unions

ROBERT C. MAYER
Woll, Mayer and St. Antoine

RUDOLF MODLEY
Editor, Reports, Inc.

WALLACE P. MORS
Professor of Finance,
Babson Institute of Business
Administration

M. R. NEIFELD
Consulting Economist

VINCENT J. NOLAN
Deputy Superintendent of Banking,
New York State Banking Department

HARLOWE OSBORNE
Senior Economist,
Office of Assistant Secretary
for Economic Affairs,
U.S. Department of Commerce

TYNAN SMITH
Associate Adviser,
Division of Research and Statistics,
Board of Governors of the Federal
Reserve System

ORVILLE K. THOMPSON
Division of Research and Statistics,
Board of Governors of the Federal
Reserve System

DONALD M. D. THURBER
Member, Board of Overseers' Committee
to Visit Harvard College

WILLIAM J. TRENT
Assistant Director of Personnel,
Time, Inc.

KENNETH WILLSON
President,
National Better Business Bureau

The research report has benefited greatly from review and constructive criticism by this committee. The conclusions finally reached, however, are those of the authors and editors.

Contents

	PAGE
Foreword	xv
Preface	xvii

I. ROLE OF CONSUMER FINANCE COMPANIES IN A CREDIT
     ECONOMY   1

   John M. Chapman

Introduction	1
The Consumer Credit Industry	2
Composition of Consumer Instalment Credit Outstanding	6
Development of Personal Cash Loans Within the	
Consumer Instalment Credit Field	11
Functions: Consumer Instalment Cash Lending Institutions	13
Competition and Diversification	14
Some Factors Affecting Costs	17
Cost Differences Among Consumer Credit Institutions	19
Acquisition Costs	22
Risk Management, Losses, and Charge-Offs	22
Overextension of Credit—Need for Counseling Service	25

II. RECENT TRENDS IN THE FINANCIAL POSITION OF NINE MAJOR
     CONSUMER FINANCE COMPANIES   29

   Paul F. Smith

Return on Consumer Receivables	31
Gross Income on Consumer Receivables	31
Operating Expenses	36
Nonoperating Expenses	41
Related Earning Activities	41
Effective Use of Total Resources	43
Return on Total Assets	45
Role of Financing in Profits	47
Profits	49

Comparison of Companies with Highest and Lowest
  Charges to Consumers   50
Comparison of Companies with Highest and Lowest
  Profit Rates   52

III. A CROSS-SECTION STUDY OF INDUSTRY COSTS AND EARNINGS   55

    Jack Zwick

  Summary of Findings   55
  The Research Method   57
  The Sample and the Data   59
  Factors Affecting Operating Costs   61
  The Evidence   63
  Operating-Cost Ratios and Average Loan Size   63
  Operating-Cost Ratios and Loan Risk   66
  Operating-Cost Ratios and Loan Mix   67
  Gross Income and Operating-Profit Relationships   68
  Gross Income Ratios and Average Loan Size   69
  Operating-Profit Ratios and Average Loan Size   71
  Operating-Profit Ratios and Loan Risk   74
  Operating-Profit Ratios and Loan Mix   79
  Operating-Profit Ratios and Number of Loans per Office 80
  Number of Loans per Office and Company Size   82
  The Assumption of Linearity   83
  Summary and Implications of the Findings   84

IV. STATE REGULATION AND THE PROVISION OF SMALL LOANS   87

    Robert P. Shay

  Introduction   87
  Summary of Findings   87
  The Basic Data and Concepts   89
  Operating Income and Cost Ratios in Thirty States   92
  Operating Ratios in Regulated Small-Loan Markets   97
  Gross Income Ratios per $100 of Average Loans
    Outstanding and per Loan Account   98
  Operating Expense Ratios per $100 Average Loans
    Outstanding and per Loan Account   102
  Net Operating Income Ratios   104
  Measuring Loan Services Under the Small-Loan Laws:
    Presence of Other Laws   105

Convenience and Advantage Clauses in Relation to
    Loan Service   112
Supplementary Insights from the Operating Ratios of the
    Four Largest Consumer Finance Companies   114
Comparative Operating Experience: Four Large
    Companies and All Companies   114

V. FACTORS AFFECTING THE COST OF BORROWING BY CONSUMER
    FINANCE COMPANIES   121

    Jack Zwick

The Cost of Borrowed Funds   122
Cost of Borrowing by Size of Company   123
Composition of Liabilities and Cost of Borrowing   125
Degree of Leverage and Borrowing Costs   133
Term Structure of Liabilities and Borrowing Costs   134
Conclusion   135

VI. CONCLUSIONS FOR REGULATION   137

    Robert W. Johnson

Ceilings on Consumer Finance Charges   139
Ceilings on Size of Credit Extensions   153
Freedom of Entry   156
Summary   161

APPENDIX 1. DESCRIPTION OF NINE-COMPANY CONSUMER
    FINANCE SAMPLE AND OF ADJUSTMENTS IN DATA   163

APPENDIX 2. CONSUMER FINANCE RATE AND REGULATION
    CHART   167

INDEX   175

Tables

PAGE

1. Comparison of the Amount of Consumer Credit Outstanding with Net Public and Private Debt: Gross National Product and Disposable Personal Income, 1939, 1949, 1959, and 1964   4

2. Consumer Instalment Credit Market by Holder, December 31, 1950, 1960, and 1964   8

3. Provision for Losses, Gross Charge-Offs, and Net Charge-Offs as Percentage of Consumer Receivables: Nine Consumer Finance Companies, 1949–64   24

4. Gross Income on Consumer Receivables, 1950–64   36

5. Components of Finance Charges on Consumer Receivables 1950–64   38

6. Range in Operating Expenses by Type of Expense, 1964   38

7. Provisions for Losses and Actual Losses, 1950–64   39

8. Distribution of Operating Expenses on Consumer Receivables by Type of Expense, 1950–64   40

9. Comparison of Net Operating Income from Consumer Receivables and from Other Sources, 1950–64   42

10. Distribution of Assets, End of Year, 1950–64   42

11. Distribution of Sources of Funds, End of Year, 1950–64   44

12. Distribution of Nine Companies by Ratio of Net Operating Income to Total Assets, 1960 and 1964   46

13. Factors Affecting Return on Total Assets, 1960–64   46

14. Cost of Nonequity Funds, 1950–64 47

15. Role of Nonequity Funds in Profits, 1950–64 48

16. Consumer Finance Company Profits, 1950–64 50

17. Factors Affecting Return of Equity, 1960–64 51

18. Comparison of Companies with Highest and Lowest Average Finance Charges, 1960–64 52

19. Comparison of Selected High- and Low-Profit Companies, 1960–64 53

20. Average Loan Size, Number of Loans Outstanding per Office, and Total Costs per $100 of Loans Outstanding 57

21. Reported Average Operating Income and Cost Data, Licensed Consumer Finance Offices in Thirty States, 1964 93

22. Selected Operating Ratios in Thirty States, 1964 100

23. Simple Associations Between Gross Income Ratios and Selected Ratios, Thirty States, 1964 102

24. Simple Associations Between Operating Expense Ratios and Selected Ratios, Thirty States, 1964 103

25. Simple Associations Between Net Operating Income Ratios and Selected Ratios, Thirty States, 1964 104

26. Ranking of States Under Alternative Measures of the Provision of Small-Loan Services and Related Statutory Provisions 108

27. Comparison of Seventeen States Ranked by Population per Office and Loans per Office with Rankings by Loan Service Measures 113

28. Comparative Operating Income and Cost Data for Licensed Consumer Finance Offices, 1964 115

29. Rank Correlations of Selected Ratios of Four Large Consumer Finance Companies, Twenty-Nine States, 1964   117

30. Selected Ratios from Data in State Reports, Thirty States, 1964   118

31. Cost of Borrowing and Burden Coverage in Percentages for Consumer Finance Sample by Size of Company, 1962–64   125

32. Liabilities of Sample Consumer Finance Companies by Size of Company, 1962–64   129

33. Senior and Subordinatetd Debt as Percentages of Total Long-Term Debt by Size of Company, 1962–64   129

34. Borrowing Ratios and Proportions for Consumer Finance Sample by Size of Company, 1962–64   130

35. Commercial Paper Issuance as Percentage of Short-Term Financing by Size of Company, 1962–64   131

36. Net Profits After Taxes to Equity Funds of Nine Major Consumer Finance Companies, Manufacturing Corporations, and Commercial Banks, 1960–64   142

37. Increase in Unit Cost per $100 Increase in Average Loan Size   149

Charts

		PAGE
1.	Growth of Consumer Instalment Credit Extensions in Relation to Consumer Expenditures for Durables and Services and Gross National Product, 1949–64	5
2.	Percentage Distribution of Total Consumer Credit Outstanding by Holder, 1950–64	9
3.	Percentage Distribution of Personal Loans Outstanding by Holder, 1950–64	10
4.	Factors in Return on Consumer Receivables, 1950–64	32
5.	Range of Return on Consumer Receivables for Nine Companies, 1950–64	33
6.	Gross Income from Consumer Receivables, 1930–41 and 1949–64	34
7.	Costs and Loans per Office	58
8.	Average Loan Size and Operating Cost Ratios, 1962–64	65
9.	Net Charge-Offs as Percentage of Average Loans Outstanding and Operating Cost Ratios, 1962–64	67
10.	Business and Sales Finance Loans as Percentage of Total Loans Outstanding and Operating Cost Ratios, 1962–64	69
11.	Average Loan Size and Gross Income per $100 of Loans Outstanding, 1962–64	70
12.	Average Loan Size and Operating Costs, Gross Income, and EBIT per $100 of Loans Outstanding, 1962–64	72

13. Portfolio Risk and Gross Income, 1962–64   75

14. Net Charge-Offs as Percentage of Average Outstandings
    and Operating Costs, Gross Income, and EBIT per $100 of
    Loans Outstanding, 1962–64   76

15. Business and Sales Finance Loans as Percentage of Total
    Loans and Gross Income per $100 of Outstandings, 1962–64   77

16. Business Loans and Sales Finance Credit as Percentage of
    Total Loans and Operating Costs, Gross Income, and EBIT
    per $100 of Outstandings, 1962–64   78

17. Number of Loans Outstanding per Office and EBIT per
    $100 of Loans Outstanding, 1962–64   81

18. Simple Correlation Between the Number of Loans Out-
    standing per Office and Company Size   82

19. Company Size and Cost of Borrowing   124

20. Company Size and Nonsubordinated Long-Term Debt as
    Percentage of Total Borrowing   126

21. Company Size and Short-Term Borrowing from Commercial
    Banks as Proportion of Total Borrowing   127

22. Company Size and Commercial Paper as Proportion of
    Total Borrowing   128

23. Comparison of New York Prime Commercial Bank Rate
    and Goldman, Sachs & Co.'s Prime Three-Month Net Rate
    of Commercial Paper Borrowers   132

24. Company Size and Long-Term Debt as Percentage of Total
    Negotiated Borrowings   136

25. Average Direct Unit Cost Curves   157

Foreword

This book is the product of the cooperative efforts of businessmen, academic scholars, and representatives of government, all with a common interest in consumer finance. This type of collaboration illustrates the kind of partnership which the Graduate School of Business of Columbia University is privileged to sponsor in order to bring objective scholarship to bear upon the pressing problems confronting business and the public at large.

Consumer credit has emerged as a major influence in the western world in the twentieth century. Its benefits in facilitating distribution and consumption are recognized even in those parts of the world that have been unable to afford such inducements to an expanding economy. As with all good things, however, there are associated hazards. As the role of consumer credit has increased in importance in the total economy, the need for objective inquiry into all of its aspects has become more urgent. The present volume represents such an inquiry; on behalf of its authors, sponsors, and the Business School, it is a pleasure to present these findings.

COURTNEY C. BROWN
Dean

Preface

The primary objectives of the study may be stated as follows: (a) to evaluate the services rendered by regulated consumer finance companies; (b) to determine and evaluate operating and nonoperating costs incurred in providing these services; (c) to appraise the effects of regulatory laws upon the performance of lenders; and (d) to suggest standards for regulating and setting rates of charge in relation to the provision of loan services.

Legislation, of course, influences the costs and kinds of services provided to borrowers. We feel that such changes in legislation should be enacted only with a full understanding of consumer credit costs. Particularly important is knowledge of trends in costs and the nature of differences in costs among companies as well as among the states in which they operate. Previous cost studies have presented useful facts and analyses of the industry. The studies for the National Bureau of Economic Research by Ernst A. Dauer and Paul F. Smith cited in the text are important examples. We have endeavored to bring as much of their information up to date as possible. Using materials supplied by the National Consumer Finance Association, we have studied cost differences among finance companies. Finally, we have made an initial effort to investigate cost data assembled and made available by the state regulatory authorities.

Legislation based on various drafts of the Russell Sage Foundation's Uniform Small Loan Law was directed primarily at two major problems: first, finding an available source of consumer credit; second, eliminating the loan-shark evil. For the past fifty years, statutes have been altered and other statutes enacted in response to special problems and needs. This piecemeal method of enacting legislation has not solved the complex problems confronting consumer finance companies and other segments of the consumer credit industry. We need coordinated and balanced legislation to facilitate the future growth of consumer credit in terms of society's needs.

The National Conference of Commissioners on Uniform State Laws have recognized the seriousness of this problem by creating a special committee to make a study to determine how present laws may be simplified and coordinated to meet the needs of both the recipients and grantors of consumer credit. We hope this study will contribute to their deliberations.

The study was made possible by research grants from sixteen finance companies. The research project was organized on the basis of original grants by six companies: American Investment Company, Associates Investment Company, Beneficial Finance Company, C.I.T. Financial Corporation, Household Finance Corporation, and the Seaboard Finance Company. After the research work was inaugurated, it was suggested that other companies might wish to join the original group. Ten welcomed the opportunity to participate. Additional grants were made to the fund by Capital Finance Company, Commercial Credit Company, The Dial Finance Company, Family Finance Corporation, General Acceptance Corporation, General Finance Corporation, Credithrift Financial Corporation, ITT Aetna Finance Corporation, Pacific Finance Corporation, and State Loan & Finance Management Corporation.

Special acknowledgments and thanks are due the members of the Advisory Committee for their assistance in formulating the plans for this research project, conferring with members of the research staff on various occasions, and attending committee meetings. Their suggestions and criticisms have been most helpful, and members of the research staff are most grateful for their cooperation.

We express our thanks to Dean Courtney C. Brown and William C. Spencer, Associate Dean, for their generous counsel and assistance in planning and organizing the project from its beginning.

We are indebted to a number of persons for their assistance in the preparation of this study. We appreciate the help of Courtney N. Blackman, Jean Dorr, and Marvin Rosenberg in assembling and compiling statistical data; Jean Dorr and Joan Rabinow, for their secretarial skills; and Mark H. Willes, research assistant, for tabulating and analyzing statistical data.

We wish to acknowledge the special assistance received from many state supervisory officials, especially Vincent J. Nolan, Deputy Superintendent of Banking, New York State.

James F. McRee edited the final draft and shepherded the manuscript through publication. H. Irving Forman prepared the charts.

We are deeply indebted to S. Lees Booth and the National Consumer Finance Association for making available to us a large body of statistical data gathered by means of its annual questionnaire to its members. We are also indebted to the following companies that provided statistical data: American Investment Company, Beneficial Finance Company, Family Finance Corporation, Household Finance Corporation, Credithrift Financial Corporation, Liberty Loan Corporation, Merchants Acceptance Corporation, Seaboard Finance Company, and State Loan & Finance Management Corporation.

JOHN M. CHAPMAN
ROBERT P. SHAY

I

Role of Consumer Finance Companies in a Credit Economy

*Graduate School of Business,
Columbia University*

Introduction

Consumer credit has been defined by the Board of Governors of the Federal Reserve System as including all short- and intermediate-term credit extended through regular business channels to finance the purchase of commodities and services for personal consumption, or to refinance debts incurred for such purposes.[1] It is divided into two major types, instalment and noninstalment, which in turn are subdivided according to both the type of credit and the class of institution to which the obligation is owed. The four principal classes of consumer instalment credit are automobile paper, other consumer goods paper, home repair and modernization loans, and personal loans. Noninstalment credit is divided into three major components: single-payment loans, charge accounts, and service credit.[2]

[1] The term consumer credit may refer either to an advance of funds for the purchase of goods or services or to an advance of goods and services, in exchange for a promise to pay at a later date.

[2] Certain types of credit extended to businesses, or to individuals and used exclusively for business purposes, credit extended to governmental agencies or to nonprofit or charitable organizations, policy loans of life insurance companies, loans by one individual to another for consumption purposes, and loans made by businesses to their employees are excluded.

1

The principal classes of financial institutions holding consumer obligations include commercial banks, sales finance companies, consumer finance companies, credit unions, and "other financial institutions."[3] Consumer finance companies, the subject of this study, are defined by the Board of Governors of the Federal Reserve System as companies engaged primarily in making consumer instalment loans and have one-half or more of their consumer receivables in loans made under an effective state small-loan law. The bulk of the credit they extend is in the form of direct personal cash loans to consumers.[4] The consumer finance industry, on the other hand, consists basically of consumer finance companies and the cash-lending subsidiaries of sales finance companies, whose operations are primarily those of licensed lenders under state small-loan laws.

The Consumer Credit Industry

The widespread and rapidly growing use of consumer instalment credit has played a significant role in our national economy during the period since World War II. The total amount of this credit outstanding rose from $11.6 billion in December 1949 to $60.5 billion on December 31, 1964, showing an annual growth rate of 11.5 per cent during the period (Table 1).

The demand for consumer instalment credit has not only expanded but has broadened during the past two or three decades. The market for it has long since passed that stage of its development and growth when its principal objective was to finance necessitous borrowers or those who wanted to purchase a sewing machine, a piece of furniture, or other household equipment under an instalment contract. Consumers are now using consumer instalment credit to obtain a variety of durable goods and services, education, travel, and so on, as well as nondurable consumer goods. Manufacturers and distributors of consumer durable goods regard consumer instalment credit as an important marketing device. The advantages to the family and to the economy through the use of consumer instal-

---

[3] The "other financial institutions" included in published data are mutual savings banks, savings and loan associations, industrial loan companies, and all other financial firms engaged in the consumer loan business but not included elsewhere in the series. Board of Governors of the Federal Reserve System, *Supplement to Banking and Monetary Statistics*, Washington, 1965, p. 13.

[4] *Ibid.*, p. 15.

ment credit have resulted in a situation in which it is common in many American families to use consumer instalment cash loans for the purchase of durable consumer goods and services and to consolidate their debts. In fact, because many families' incomes are too low for private lenders to risk financing them, the federal government is seeking ways and means out of this dilemma.

The growing demand for consumer instalment credit by consumers to purchase durable consumer goods and services can be accounted for largely by the growth in population, earlier family formation, rising incomes, and the increasing availability of sources for consumer credit. The existence of hospital and medical insurance, unemployment insurance, pension funds, and social security helps to protect the consumer against interruptions in his income and gives him greater ability to incur debts.

The increased importance of consumer instalment credit may also be emphasized by comparing its expansion with the increase in the gross national product, the changes in personal disposable income, and the rise in expenditures for durable consumer goods and services (see Chart 1 and Table 1).

The Board of Governors of the Federal Reserve System stressed the importance of consumer credit in stimulating production and employment in part as follows:

Consumer credit is thus an important means of financing the flow of goods and services into final consumption and is a factor influencing the level of economic activity. Over long periods of generally rising activity the extension of credit to purchasers of consumer goods has supplemented current purchasing power, and this has tended to stimulate production and employment. But substantial increases in consumer purchasing power through the extension of credit in periods of high economic activity are appropriate only when the terms on which credit is extended are prudent, the growth of such credit does not contribute excessively to monetary expansion, and when the new purchasing power is matched by an increase in the supply of goods at relatively stable prices.[5]

The expansion of consumer instalment credit has been accompanied by corresponding development in other factors or characteristics of the consumer credit industry. Consumers have widened their use of consumer credit in acquiring consumer capital goods. More people are also using consumer instalment credit because they enjoy larger incomes and steady employment. Financial institutions have modified

[5] *Ibid.*, p. 1.

TABLE 1

Comparison of the Amount of Consumer Credit Outstanding with Net Public and Private Debt: Gross National Product and Disposable Personal Income, 1939, 1949, 1959, and 1964

(dollar amounts in billions)

	Amount Outstanding				Percentage Increase		
	1939	1949	1959	1964	1939-49	1949-59	1959-64
A. Form of Debt							
Business[a]	83.4	131.9	312.0	447.5	58.2	136.5	43.4
Farm mortgages	8.8	12.0	23.0	35.7	36.4	91.7	55.2
Nonfarm mortgages	25.0	50.6	160.8	259.3[c]	102.4	217.8	61.2
Consumer credit, total[b]	7.2	17.4	51.5	78.4[d]	141.7	196.0	52.2
State and local	16.3	18.1	55.6	85.2	11.0	207.2	53.2
Federal government net	42.6	218.4	243.2	267.2	413.1	11.4	9.9
Total	183.3	448.4	846.1	1173.3	144.6	88.7	38.7
B. Gross national product	90.5	256.5	483.7	628.7	183.4	88.6	30.1
C. Consumer instalment credit	4.5	11.6	39.2	60.5	157.8	237.9	54.3
D. Disposable personal income	70.3	188.6	337.3	435.8	168.3	78.8	29.2

Source: Net public and private debt, *Economic Report of the President, 1966*, p. 272, and Federal Reserve Board.

[a] The term business debt as used here includes corporate long- and short-term debt ($401.7 billion) and noncorporate commercial and financial debt ($45.8 billion) for 1964.

[b] The amount of consumer instalment credit outstanding is shown in line C above. It is included also in "consumer credit, total."

[c] Total nonfarm mortgage debt of $259.3 billion consists of $187.0 billion on 1- to 4-family homes and $72.3 billion of other nonfarm mortgages.

[d] The total amount of consumer credit was given as $76.8 billion in the *Economic Report of the President, 1966*, p. 272. The revised estimates of consumer credit outstanding for 1964 by the Federal Reserve Board increased the total to $78.4 billion, making a difference between the two totals of $1.6 billion. (See *Federal Reserve Bulletin*, May 1964 pp. 736-738.) The increase in consumer credit raises the total amount of net public and private from $1,171.7 billion to $1,173.3.

CHART 1

**Growth of Consumer Instalment Credit Extensions
in Relation to Consumer Expenditures for Durables and
Services and Gross National Product, 1949–64**

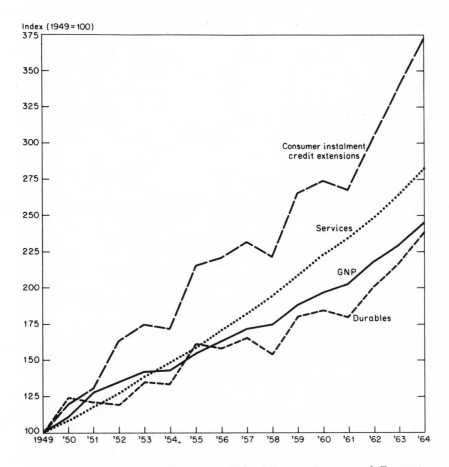

SOURCE: Department of Commerce, Federal Reserve System, and *Economic Report of the President*, 1964.

their field of activity, and have changed their terms and methods in meeting the needs and requirements of consumers in a changing economy. Perhaps attention should be called to the fact that a number of economists and writers on this subject feel that the extension of consumer instalment credit has caused some public concern about the amount outstanding. It is generally conceded, however, that consumer instalment credit has made a marked contribution to the growth of our national economy.[6]

Another indication of the relative magnitude of consumer instalment credit in our national economy is presented in Table 1, which shows the amount of the outstanding debt for each of the six major types of net public and private debt for each of four different years (1939, 1949, 1959, and 1964). Consumer debt[7] represented 6.6 per cent of the total debt outstanding in 1964 as compared with 3.9 per cent of the total for 1949 and 3.9 per cent for 1939. The relative rate of growth for given periods of time may be seen by reference to Chart 1 and Table 1. The growth during the period 1959–64 for non-mortgage debt,[8] farm mortgage debt, and total consumer credit rose 61, 55, and 52 per cent respectively. Consumer instalment debt increased 54 per cent during the same period. The gross national product rose 30 per cent and disposable personal income only 29 per cent. It is important to observe that if a longer period of time were taken, the percentage variations would have been greater.

Composition of Consumer Instalment Credit Outstanding

Consumer instalment credit typically takes the form of either retail instalment financing or instalment loans. The Federal Reserve Board,

[6] *Ibid.*, pp. 1–2.

[7] Total consumer credit outstanding amounted to $78.4 billion as of December 31, 1964. Of this amount, $60.5 (or 77 per cent) represented consumer instalment credit. The balance, $17.9 billion (or 23 per cent), was noninstalment credit. Consumer debt as used here refers to both instalment and noninstalment consumer credit.

[8] There has been an important development in refinancing mortgage indebtedness by commercial banks and savings banks to provide funds for current consumption purposes. Mr. A has a home on which the mortgage has been reduced by regular periodical payments from $15,000 to $5,000. By refinancing he may increase the original mortgage to $12,000, thus making available to him the difference, or $7,000, with which he may purchase an automobile, take a trip to Europe, increase his bank balance, or use the funds for a variety of current purposes. For a fuller discussion of this type of financing, see National Industrial Conference Board, *New Dimension in Mortgage Debt,* New York, July 1964.

in preparing its estimates of the amount of consumer instalment credit outstanding has presented the total in two different ways: (1) by type of credit, classified according to indicated purposes or security, and (2) by holder of the receivables.

As stated earlier, consumer instalment credit is divided into four categories: credit used to purchase automobiles, credit used to purchase other goods, credit used for repair and modernization of homes, and personal cash loans. The first three categories include direct loans from lenders as well as credit contracts originated by retailers who either hold or sell their retail paper to financial institutions: the fourth represents the remaining cash loans. Each constitutes a distinct market for consumer instalment credit. The relative portion of each category is shown by its percentage share of the total amount of consumer instalment credit at any given time. The amount outstanding on December 31, 1964, was $60.5 billion, of which 41.6 per cent represented automobile credit, 25.8 per cent credit for other durables, 5.8 per cent repair and moderization, and 26.8 per cent personal loans.

Since the remainder of this chapter deals primarily with problems and questions concerning costs incurred by regulated finance companies, it seems desirable to see how large a portion the consumer finance companies held of the total amount of consumer instalment credit outstanding[9] and the total amount of personal cash instalment loans outstanding. Table 2 presents these amounts for each of the principal financial institutions which held the bulk of the consumer instalment credit outstanding at the end of 1964.

Actually, on December 31, 1964, the consumer finance companies held 8.4 per cent of the total amount of consumer credit and 27.3 per cent of the total amount of personal cash instalment loans outstanding. Chart 2 and Table 2 show the trends of each of the primary holders of the total amount of consumer instalment credit outstanding for the period 1950–64. Commercial banks and credit unions gradually increased their shares of total instalment consumer credit from 1950 to 1964, while each of the other types of holders sustained a decline.

Chart 3 indicates the trend for each of the four main holders of the amount of personal cash instalment loans outstanding.[10] It registers a small percentage increase for commercial banks from about 1957 to 1964. The percentage holdings of credit unions and sales finance com-

[9] It should be noted that cash lending subsidiaries of sales finance companies are to all intents and purposes the same as a consumer finance company.

[10] Personal cash instalment loans constitute a large share of the total outstandings held by consumer finance companies.

TABLE 2
Consumer Instalment Credit Market by Holder,
December 31, 1950, 1960, and 1964
(dollar amounts in billions)

	1950		1960		1964	
	Amount	Per Cent	Amount	Per Cent	Amount	Per Cent
I. Total Consumer Instalment Credit						
Sales finance companies	3.7	25.2	11.4	26.8	14.8	24.4
Consumer finance companies	1.3	8.7	3.7	8.6	5.1	8.4
Commercial banks	5.8	39.4	16.7	38.9	25.1	41.4
Credit unions[a]	.6	4.0	3.9	9.2	6.4	10.7
Other financial institutions[a]	.4	3.0	1.5	3.4	1.7	2.9
Total financial institutions	11.8	80.3	37.2	86.9	53.1	87.8
Retailers	2.9	19.7	5.6	13.1	7.4	12.2
Total	14.7	100.0	42.8	100.0	60.5	100.0
II. Personal Cash Instalment Loans						
Sales finance companies	.16	5.8	1.07	10.2	2.03	12.5
Consumer finance companies	1.03	36.7	3.13	29.8	4.44	27.3
Total consumer finance industry	1.19	42.5	4.20	40.0	6.47	39.8
Commercial banks	1.04	36.8	3.58	34.1	5.54	34.2
Credit unions[a]	.37	13.2	1.97	18.8	3.24	20.0
Other financial institutions[a]	.21	7.5	.73	7.1	.97	6.0
Total	2.81	100.0	10.48	100.0	16.22	100.0

Source: Board of Governors of the Federal Reserve System, Release G.22.
[a] Separate estimates of the holdings of credit unions and "other" financial institutions provided by Ernst A. Dauer, Household Finance Corporation.

CHART 2

Percentage Distribution of Total Consumer Credit Outstanding by Holder, 1950–64

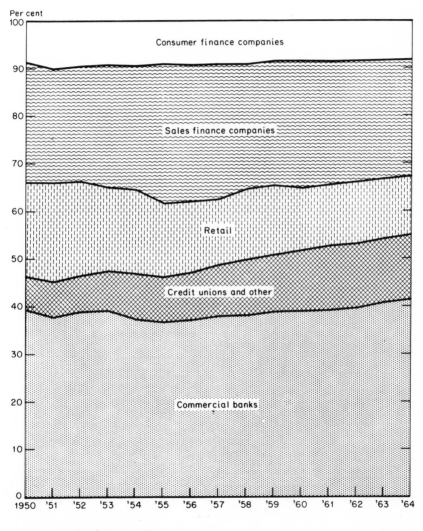

SOURCE: Federal Reserve System.

CHART 3

Percentage Distribution of Personal Loans Outstanding by Holder, 1950–64

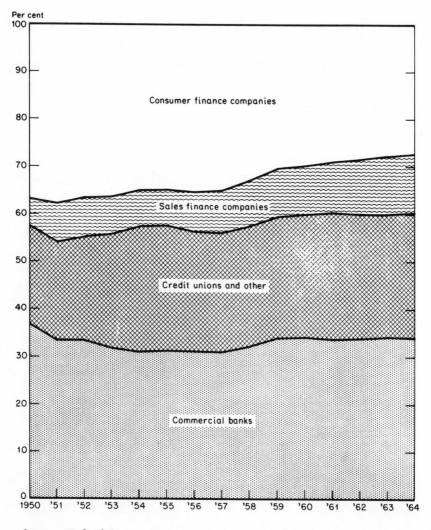

SOURCE: Federal Reserve System.

panies show modest increases, but consumer finance companies declined from 35.1 to 27.3 per cent of the total amount of personal cash instalment loans. It is clear that consumer finance companies held a relatively small segment of the total consumer instalment credit outstanding and a much larger part of total personal instalment loans outstanding. However, the importance of the part played by the consumer finance industry is not determined by consumer finance companies alone because cash-lending subsidiaries of sales finance companies increased their share of the personal instalment loan market.[11]

In evaluating their contribution, it is necessary to keep in mind the fact that a large part of the loans made by these companies is extended to borrowers who rely more or less exclusively on this source of credit. Regardless of the total amount involved, consumer finance companies perform a unique function in the consumer credit market by making loans available to higher risk borrowers who rely heavily on personal loans for emergencies as well as for the purchase of consumer goods and services. For many borrowers they are the lenders of last resort.

Development of Personal Cash Loans Within the Consumer Instalment Credit Field

By the turn of the century, urban wage earners and other individuals with low incomes were in need of consumer credit to bridge the gap between income and expenditures.[12] Consumers found it difficult, if not impossible, to obtain such loans at reasonable rates.[13] The costs of acquiring and servicing small cash loans were so high that most lenders could not make consumer loans at the legal rate without suf-

[11] See Table 2, part II.

[12] Cash lending agencies, pawnbrokers, and note shavers were active in this area of credit prior to the Civil War. Pawnbrokers made cash loans to consumers and received pledges in the form of tangible personal property. The pledges included clothing, watches, and jewelry. Note shavers granted credit to small businessmen on equipment and inventories; to farmers on livestock, buildings, and crops; to craftsmen and salaried employees on houses and other security. Note shavers received notes bearing the maximum legal rate of interest and, in addition, commissions and charges for services and expenses. Rolf Nugent, *Consumer Credit and Economic Stability*, New York, 1939, pp. 57–60.

[13] Evidently some progress had been made toward the development of facilities for financing small loans. "Successful lenders organized chain systems of offices and by this means the business was soon extended to industrial communities

source of credit for small-loan borrowers, many of whom had been exploited by loan sharks. Around 1909 or 1910, credit unions were authorized by various state laws to promote thrift and provide borrowing facilities for members, who were also composed largely of low-income salary and wage earners.

Both consumer finance companies and credit unions were authorized by state laws to make personal cash loans for "provident and productive purposes" to wage earners and other low-income borrowers who had little, if any, access to other sources of credit.[18] A basic difference between the two types of financial institutions should be recognized. The consumer finance companies approach their potential borrowers as members of the public at large; credit unions regard the same potential borrowers as members of a small coherent group to which they belong (for example, as employees, church members, fraternity members, teachers).

Commercial banks were originally established and developed to issue notes, receive deposits, and make loans primarily to industrial and commercial concerns. In the late 1920's and the 1930's a number of commercial banks entered the field of consumer instalment credit. Sales finance companies were established originally to make business loans, especially short-term loans to wholesalers and manufacturers. Following 1915, sales finance companies took on new life when they began to purchase dealers' automobile paper and to make wholesale loans for financing inventories and the purchasing of durable goods by their customers.

If each of these various types of financial institutions had confined its operations to the purposes originally envisioned, it would have meant that each type would have been highly specialized. In fact, during the decade 1910–20 and for some years thereafter, these financial institutions restricted their operations basically to the type of lending in the area for which they were created, after which they began to diversify.

Competition and Diversification

Prior to 1935, the consumer finance companies encountered relatively little competition in their specialized field. With the decline of

---

[18] Development of both types of institutions was encouraged by the work of the Russell Sage Foundation.

specialization among financial institutions in the field of consumer credit, however, competition increased. It became a more significant force in the consumer credit business in the 1950's. There is widespread and growing interest in competition, not only among consumer finance companies, which are still engaged basically in making personal cash loans, but also among the other types of financial institutions that entered the consumer credit field. Competition is specially marked among the four principal types of financial institutions— commercial banks, sales finance companies, consumer finance companies, and credit unions—which provide the major share of consumer instalment credit used by consumers at the present time. Current developments taking place in the consumer credit market suggest that the consumer credit business will become more and more competitive in the future.

Effective competition raises some very complicated problems. Different types of financial agencies do not operate under a uniform law. There is a great lack of uniformity of laws governing operations of different types of institutions within a given state, not to mention the still greater variations among different states. Ceilings on finance charges and size of loans to individual borrowers vary widely from one type of financial institution to another and they tend to limit their operations to different classes of credit risk. These differences are most marked between consumer finance companies and commercial banks. The higher finance charges of the consumer finance companies enable them to make "higher-risk" loans than those ordinarily made by commercial banks and credit unions. Not only do finance charges and permitted loan sizes differ among types of financial institutions; there are also differences in the nature and number of services, maturities, cost of funds, necessity of keeping records, losses or net chargeoffs, and other factors, including free or low occupancy costs and tax exemptions.

Each of the financial agencies has been pushing aggressively for new business in personal cash loans as well as in consumer credit generally. As these financial institutions gain greater penetration through expansion and diversification, they compete more aggressively. In endeavoring to enlarge its volume of business, each type of financial agency has stressed the area where it has the greatest potential advantage. To illustrate briefly, commercial banks emphasize low interest rates and larger loans; credit unions point out that they make loans only to members and at lower rates and for larger amounts than some of their competitors. Consumer finance companies, in turn, stress convenience and availability of service, as well as the ability to offer higher-risk loans than their competitors.

It may not always be easy to determine whether a given policy or program of a corporation grows out of a desire to expand or to diversify. Both elements are usually present. Frequently, it is desirable to diversify as a part of a program of expansion. This situation would seem to be present at this time with regard to sales finance companies. Competitive forces are stronger today then ever before in the consumer credit market. How to deal in the future with the interrelationships of growth, competition, and diversification of financial institutions raises some important problems which cannot safely be ignored.

Competition has led to an increase in mergers and consolidations among existing institutions. The belief is held in some quarters that if consumer finance companies were given more permissive legislation with higher loan ceilings, they could, by skillful operations and able management, continue to maintain their share of a profitable consumer finance business. Mutual savings banks and savings and loan associations, now generally limited by law, are anxious to expand their consumer credit business. If either or both groups are permitted to do so, no doubt competition will be greatly intensified.

Despite the fact that consumer finance companies as a group have continued their heavy specialization in personal loans, there are indications that important changes have been taking place, especially during the 1960's. Two of the largest of our sample of nine major consumer companies have entered the retailing business on an important scale. Another company has purchased a furniture business, some have entered the field of commercial financing, wholesale financing is being carried on by some companies, and the insurance business is becoming more common as well. These changes suggest important developments, even though consumer financing still accounts for a large percentage of the total business being carried on by consumer finance companies. "The participation of the nine companies in outside activities ranged widely from one company that reported only 1.3 per cent of its net operating income from nonconsumer sources to another that reported 28 per cent from such sources."[19]

For the membership of National Consumer Finance Association, personal loans as a percentage of accounts and notes receivable held by consumer finance companies dropped from 87 per cent in 1960 to 84 per cent in 1964. Retail auto credit rose from 1 per cent of the total

[19] See Chapter II, p. 43.

in 1960 to 4 per cent in 1964.[20] Income from consumer receivables accounted for 94 per cent of the total in 1960 as compared with 85 per cent in 1964. Income other than that obtained from consumer business accounted for 6 per cent of the total gross income in 1960 as compared to 15 per cent in 1964.[21] There has been a gradual increase of dual business among consumer finance companies.

Paul F. Smith, discussing the period 1949–59, concluded that consumer finance companies "have increased their activities in business areas other than lending to consumers." Investment in nonconsumer earning assets averaged about 1.5 per cent of the total assets through the 1950's. In bringing his earlier study down to the end of 1964, Smith notes that "this figure had doubled by 1960, and increased to 6.4 per cent of the total by the end of 1964." This trend can be observed even more clearly in the proportion of net operating income received from insurance and nonconsumer activities. The ratio of net operating income from nonconsumer activities to the total averaged 7.5 per cent throughout the 1950's. In 1960 this ratio increased to 9.4 per cent and reached 15.8 per cent in 1964.[22]

Regardless of the original purposes underlying the organization of each type of financial institution, there is a strong tendency for each to extend its financial operations into other areas of the consumer credit business in order to enlarge its volume of business and to increase its net income.

Some Factors Affecting Costs

An objective analysis of the costs of the consumer finance business is of economic and social importance for three reasons: (1) the industry makes personal loans to high-risk borrowers and provides financial advice; (2) the services rendered are of major significance to our national economy; and (3) the industry is subject to extensive regulation in performing its services and in recovering the costs for its services. One purpose of the laws and regulations governing the consumer finance industry is to enable many consumers to obtain cash loans at a charge which is reasonable relative to the risks assumed and the costs involved. Many borrowers do not enjoy a good credit

[20] National Consumer Finance Association, *Research Report on Finance Companies in 1964*, Washington, 1964, p. 1.

[21] *Ibid.*, p. 3.

[22] *Infra*, Chapter II, Tables 9 and 10.

rating or own assets that would enable them to obtain a loan from other lenders.

The largest number of borrowers from consumer finance companies come from the skilled and unskilled wage-earner groups. White-collar workers, clerks, teachers, and civil service employees make up the next largest category. Family incomes of consumer finance company borrowers are somewhat below the median for all families ($5,747 vs. $6,569 in 1964).[23] During 1965 over 13,000,000 cash loans were made by the finance companies.[24] In 1964 the average-size loan made by the industry was about $539.[25]

The present study identifies many facts about the costs of instalment consumer credit. Two of these which should be mentioned are, first, costs tend to rise when credit standards are lowered due to the higher risk assumed by the lender; second, consumer finance companies which make relatively "higher-risk" loans tend to realize a lower net operating income than other consumer finance companies with more conservative risk exposure. These findings must be considered in the light of two additional implications: (1) services similar to those provided by consumer finance companies cannot be rendered profitably by other consumer lending agencies (or financial institutions) which operate under lower finance charges based on limited services and strict selectivity of risk; (2) numerous loan applicants have been and will continue to be rejected by lenders as submarginal risks.[26] The question is, "Would it be in the public interest to authorize higher finance charges to enable consumer finance companies to serve a larger number of those who are now being rejected?" Or are finance charges in some cases already permitting services to borrowers who would be better off without them?[27]

It is not within the scope of this study to answer the foregoing

[23] National Consumer Finance Association, *1966 Finance Facts Yearbook,* Washington, p. 51.

[24] *Ibid.,* p. 2.

[25] *Ibid.,* p. 55.

[26] See *infra,* page 22.

[27] Consumer finance companies have learned by experience that a majority of their customers have financial and credit problems which require the help of trained personnel to obtain the necessary information, to analyze it, and to find, if possible, a solution for the problems facing the customer. Counseling the family on how to manage its income usually follows the credit analysis. The evaluation of the creditworthiness should be accurate and thorough before the company decides whether to assume the risk of a loan, whether the applicant's best interests call for a loan, or whether his financial position will permit repayment.

questions, but some large consumer finance companies have for some years found it necessary to reject more than half of their new loan applicants, many of whom become prime prospects for loan sharks. There are substantial numbers of persons, largely excluded from America's legitimate credit economy, who show increasing interest in measures designed to make them eligible for credit.

Since consumer finance costs are closely related to the provision of such services, it should be emphasized that the higher rates of charge must cover the higher costs of the services which are provided in addition to the cost of money. To attract capital, it is also necessary to provide a profit related to the degree of risk assumed by the lender.

Since a great many necessitous borrowers cannot obtain loans from lenders other than consumer finance companies, one might ask whether finance charges provide a profit similar to that earned by other types of companies which compete with consumer finance companies for equity funds.[28] The nine large consumer finance companies which held 66 per cent of all consumer finance receivables in 1964 showed net profits of 12.2 per cent of equity funds,[29] as compared with 11.4 per cent for all private manufacturing corporations (*Economic Report of the President*, 1966, p. 285) and 8.8 per cent for member banks (*Federal Reserve Bulletin*, May 1965, p. 661) for the same year. During the period 1960–64, inclusive, the average net profits for each of these three types of institutions were 11.9 per cent for nine finance companies, 9.8 per cent for all private manufacturing companies, and 9.2 per cent for member banks.[30] Although the data are not fully comparable, they do suggest that large consumer finance companies do not on the average make profits that are importantly out of line with other classes of business in view of the heavy risk involved in making such loans; nor are the borrowers being charged rates which are producing net income in excess of that needed to meet the competitive costs of attracting and holding equity funds.

Cost Differences Among Consumer Credit Institutions

The finance charges obtained and the costs incurred in making consumer instalment loans differ greatly among the various types of con-

[28] Paul F. Smith, *Consumer Credit Costs, 1949–59*, Princeton, 1964, p. 96.
[29] See Chapter II, Table 16.
[30] See Chapter VI, Table 36.

sumer financing institutions. The differences in operating expenses reported paid on salaries, acquisition costs, and advertising by commercial banks, consumer finance companies, or credit unions are quite marked.[31]

Smith pointed out the variations in the gross finance charge for each of the four major types[32] of consumer credit agencies for 1959, which were stated (dollars per each $100 of average outstanding credit for the year) as follows:

Consumer finance companies	$24.04	Commercial banks	$10.04
Sales finance companies	$16.59	Credit unions	$ 9.13

NOTE: For more recent years, see Chapter 2 of this study. Unfortunately, similar data for the other three types of financial institutions are not available for the period following 1959.

Total operating expenses decreased with the height of income charges and ranged from $14.25 for consumer finance companies to $3.30 for credit unions. Nonoperating expenses ranged from $9.62 for consumer finance companies to $5.25 for commercial banks.[33]

The characteristics of the finance services rendered and the borrowers served affect markedly the relative costs to the consumer finance companies as compared with the costs of other types of lending institutions. Since the average size of the consumer instalment loans extended by the companies is smaller than the average loan size of commercial banks, they must make a larger number of loans than the banks for a given amount of loans. When costs per loan rather than costs per dollar of credit are compared, consumer finance company costs more closely approximate those of other lenders. Because the customers of consumer finance companies tend to be more highly concentrated in industrial centers, company offices tend to locate within such population concentrations, with the result that some operating costs are higher than they might be in offices located in smaller towns and rural districts. Yet the advantages of the larger number of loans per office in the larger population centers appear to more than offset the higher dollar cost per loan—resulting in lower costs per dollar of credit outstanding.

[31] Smith, *Consumer Credit Costs,* p. 96.

[32] *Ibid.,* p. 83.

[33] For a comparison of the variation in costs among the four types of financial institutions, see *ibid.,* p. 78.

There are also marked differences in the competitive aspects of consumer finance companies and credit unions. Consumer finance companies may legally charge higher rates of finance charges than credit unions. Without this privilege, consumer finance companies would be forced to raise their credit standards, which would, in turn, reduce considerably the number of wage earners who could obtain consumer instalment loans. Credit unions lend only to their own members, while consumer finance companies rely on the public at large for potential borrowers. Credit unions make larger average-sized loans, have exemptions from income taxes and receive indirect subsidies through generally lower occupancy costs and payroll deductions which curtail delinquency and limit losses. Consumer finance companies reject a larger number of their applications for new loans, which increases acquisition costs. Collection costs and charge-offs are larger for consumer finance companies than for credit unions. Since risk is a relative factor, an identical borrower might be a much better risk for a credit union than for a consumer finance company because the creditor has the advantages of a requirement for membership in a group with some common tie along with payroll deductions generally.

It may be pointed out that there are some striking differences in the competitive aspects between commercial banks and consumer finance companies. The commercial banks have larger average-sized loans, impose more stringent credit standards, and do not serve as many borrowers with low budgets. Many borrowers served by consumer finance companies are not acceptable to banks. In addition to the above-listed differences, consumer finance companies very probably rejected a larger proportion of applicants and certainly experienced larger net charge-offs, more delinquencies, and larger losses on loans made.

These various differences do not necessarily prove that some commercial bank borrowers and some finance company borrowers could not be served effectively by either type of institution. Yet they do suggest that on balance different classes of credit risks are accepted.

The obvious conclusion to draw from this discussion is that it would be wholly unrealistic to argue that finance charges should be the same for all consumer credit agencies. Much depends upon the type of loans involved as well as the borrowers themselves. In a competitive market, the finance charge must bear a close relationship to the cost of providing the services needed.

Acquisition Costs

Since the costs of acquiring new consumer loans are intermingled with other expense data, it is not possible to present specific cost data which would constitute an exact measure of the cost of acquiring new business. However, there are some facts that suggest the importance of acquisition costs. Consumer finance companies make smaller-sized loans on the average than most other consumer credit agencies. This means that acquisition costs tend to be higher per dollar of loans for these companies than other consumer financing institutions.

Another factor of importance is associated with the greater risk assumed by consumer finance companies by reason of the lower average credit rating of their applicants. Finance companies must receive and process a relatively larger number of applications, which means larger acquisition costs per loan made. It should also be noted that the larger the number of less desirable applications, the greater the number of loan applications rejected.

To obtain a more specific indication of the extent to which consumer finance companies rejected loan applicants, we requested five large- and medium-sized consumer finance companies with more than $2.75 billion of consumer receivables at the end of 1964 to give us definite information on this point.[34] Their reports showed that they rejected slightly more than 50 per cent of all new applications for the period 1957–64. The average percentage of rejections was highest (54 per cent) in 1958 and lowest (50 per cent) in 1959. The range of rejections per company in 1964 varied from 41 per cent to 66 per cent of all new applications received.

Risk Management, Losses, and Charge-Offs

Risk management by financial institutions involves broad social implications as well as possible company losses and charge-offs. For example, if the management of consumer finance companies decided to reduce the risk in making consumer instalment loans by raising credit standards, the action would decrease substantially the number of borrowers who could obtain loans from this source. Conversely, if

---

[34] Information received directly from the five companies.

management lowered its credit standards, there would be concern lest the lack of thorough credit analysis by some financial institutions would foster the use of credit by too many high-risk borrowers, resulting in increased loss ratios by consumer finance companies, adding to expenses, and resulting in recourse to bankruptcy.

The skillful evaluation of risk is essential to the success of the consumer finance industry. The successful limitation of risk in the field affects the national economy and the flow of credit to individuals. Such management policies become, as will be seen, a major factor in determining the level of operating costs of the companies. Consequently, the sound appraisal of risk affects borrowers, lenders, and the equity owners of these companies since policies and decisions on the degree of risk to be assumed affect profitability.

The approaches to credit management by a variety of institutions offering consumer instalment credit necessarily differ. Some who sell goods and credit jointly may more easily accept borrowers without a thorough investigation of their ability to repay. Others, such as commercial banks, are highly selective in accepting loan applications. For the high-risk loan applications received by consumer finance companies, it is clear that credit analysis is of vital importance in determining which borrowers may obtain loans.

Consumer finance companies have been referred to frequently as "lenders of last resort." This implies that a substantial number of consumer credit borrowers apply to consumer finance companies for loans because they believe their chances will be more favorable with these companies than with most other consumer credit agencies. These loan applications require greater attention, thus increasing costs.

Another characteristic of risk management by consumer finance companies is the follow-up or supervision of the loans after they have been made. This is especially important in view of the economic status of borrowers that they accept. Loans made by consumer finance companies are seldom secured by adequate collateral. Finance companies do not have payroll deductions, which are available generally to credit unions. They do not have the opportunity of credit merchants to cover their costs of risk by raising the cash price of the goods sold. A distinctive feature of a consumer finance company operation is a sound, aggressive collection policy the success of which will depend upon (1) a shrewd evaluation of the risk before the loans are approved, and (2) working closely with the consumer after the loans have been made.

Losses and charge-offs for consumer finance companies are necessarily greater than the losses reported by commercial banks and larger

TABLE 3

Provision for Losses, Gross Charge-Offs, and Net Charge-Offs as Percentage
of Consumer Receivables: Nine Consumer Finance Companies, 1949–64
(dollars in millions)

Year	Consumer Receivables	Provision for Losses	Provision for Losses as percentage of Consumer Receivables	Gross Charge-Offs	Gross Charge-Offs as Percentage of Consumer Receivables	Net Charge-Offs	Net Charge-Offs as Percentage of Consumer Receivables
1949	550	9	1.6	7	1.3	6	1.1
1950	704	10	1.4	7	1.0	6	.8
1951	842	12	1.4	9	1.1	6	.7
1952	1015	14	1.4	11	1.1	9	.9
1953	1144	16	1.4	13	1.1	11	1.0
1954	1223	16	1.3	16	1.3	14	1.1
1955	1419	19	1.3	16	1.1	12	.8
1956	1716	21	1.2	18	1.0	15	.9
1957	1896	26	1.4	25	1.3	22	1.2
1958	1969	33	1.7	35	1.8	32	1.6
1959	2259	35	1.5	35	1.5	30	1.3
1960	2620	51	1.9	42	1.6	37	1.4
1961	2816	51	1.8	55	2.0	48	1.7
1962	3058	56	1.8	55	1.8	47	1.5
1963	3417	62	1.8	60	1.8	51	1.5
1964	3786	66	1.7	64	1.7	54	1.4

than those reported by sales finance companies and credit unions. Consumer finance companies (like commercial banks, sales finance companies, and credit unions) have recognized the need for setting up adequate reserves, especially in view of the higher risk assumed. At the end of 1964, the nine companies in the sample reported that their consumer receivables outstanding amounted to nearly $3.8 billion (see Table 3). During that year these companies made provisions for losses amounting to nearly $66 million, or 1.7 per cent of total consumer receivables outstanding at year end. Gross charge-offs amounted to $64 million, or 97 per cent of the amount provided for losses in 1964. Net charge-offs amounted to $54 million, or 1.4 per cent of consumer receivables outstanding at the end of the year. It is evident that the companies have in recent years assumed added risks and the added costs incident to the servicing and management of such risks, as has been indicated earlier.

Overextension of Credit—Need for Counseling Service

Persons who become overextended in the use of consumer instalment credit, whether or not they become bankrupt, present a serious risk problem to consumer credit institutions, especially to consumer finance companies, since almost one half the number of personal loans made in 1964 were to consolidate existing debts.[35] The high rejection rate among new loan applicants to these companies testifies to creditors' desire to limit overextensions of credit and lessen consequent losses. As a legal lender of last resort before bankruptcy, it is important that the consumer finance companies provide effective assistance to distressed borrowers.   .

A recent study of causes of personal bankruptcy reveals the need for financial counseling service as a means of controlling the problem of overextension of consumer personal cash credit.[36] Some of the points cited are (1) individuals who finally petitioned for bankruptcy accumulated more debt at a faster rate during the twelve months preceding bankruptcy than before; (2) the purchase of goods, optional or deferrable in nature, predominated; (3) lack of financial planning and self-restraint was apparent; (4) the competitive nature of the credit market led to a relaxation of credit extension standards, resulting in inability to pay on the part of some individuals; and (5) 49 per cent of the bankruptcies studied could have paid their creditors in full, while maintaining an adequate standard of living, if given additional time and some specialized attention. Such attention should assume the form of money-management information, budget-making, and consumer education.

There is a growing trend among businessmen, acting in concert with such groups as educators, labor, family counseling, and legal aid, to establish financial credit counseling services in various communities which make available free financial advice and counsel to distressed debtors. The success of the service will depend to a large extent upon the ability and training of counselors to aid and advise debtors in the preparation of budgets and in the management of debtors' income. The abuses heaped upon citizens who are having financial difficulties by some corrupt "pro-raters" and "debt adjusters or debt poolers"

---

[35] Robert Dolphin, Jr., *An Analysis of Economic and Personal Factors Leading to Consumer Bankruptcy,* East Lansing, Mich., 1965, p. 109.

[36] *Ibid.,* pp. 95, 112.

under the pretense of helping those in financial trouble emphasize the need for the organization and functioning of financial counseling services.

Community financial counseling services should not be confused with the advice and help rendered by consumer finance companies in receiving and processing applications for personal loans. The consumer finance company is an interested party making loans to eligible applicants, but this is not the same as advice and counsel given by the community service to individuals who are in financial trouble. Often, both services may complement one another successfully to avoid the necessity for personal bankruptcies.

The overextension of consumer instalment credit is related to the rapid growth in personal bankruptcies. The number of these bankruptcies filed in the United States for the fiscal year ending June 30, 1964, totaled 155,182, an increase of 251 per cent over the number for a similar period ten years earlier.

The increasing number of personal bankruptcies suggests the existence of a growing group of overextended debtors whose lack of financial knowledge and self-discipline has created a dangerous situation for themselves as well as high collection costs for the institutions which have granted credit. Some of the distressed debtors have the desire to pay; others appear to have turned to bankruptcy as a way of getting out of trouble.[37] Competition has been a factor in some cases, especially where creditors have lowered credit standards to expand their business. There is no one cause for these conditions; neither is there an easy solution to the problem.

---

[37] "Credit counseling service on a free or nominal fee basis, which would be available to all financially distressed individuals, should be established by businessmen in all communities. Such a service was pioneered by Capital Finance Company of Columbus, Ohio, and has recently been established in many cities as cooperative effort of the business community. The counseling service provides the individual with financial help which is not available otherwise. This help may vary from advice to actual arrangement with the creditor for reduced payments over an extended period of time in more severe cases. Many individuals who otherwise go into bankruptcy could solve their problems with this type of assistance. Detailed information on the operations and methods of establishing a credit counseling service is available through the National Foundation for Consumer Credit.

"However, there are always many who could pay cash with the help of a counseling service but who would prefer to discharge their debts in bankruptcy. For this group access to bankruptcy needs to be denied." Dolphin, *Factors Leading to Consumer Bankruptcy*, p. 113.

Programs in schools, in adult educational activities, and in the use of materials received from commercial banks and credit unions represent other steps being taken to lessen bankruptcies. The American Bar Association[38] is studying ways to improve bankruptcy procedures to discourage quick bankruptcies and allow individuals to work their way out of debt over a period of time. Such public and community assistance is vitally needed to offset a problem which tends to grow with the growth of a credit economy. Some pioneering work is being done in this area under the federal Anti-Poverty Program. The National Foundation for Consumer Credit has been active in assisting the formation of a number of counseling services which are making substantial progress.

[38] The Brookings Institution has inaugurated a broad research program on bankruptcies.

II

Recent Trends in the Financial Position of Nine Major Consumer Finance Companies

PAUL F. SMITH

Wharton School of Finance and Commerce,
University of Pennsylvania

The growth of the consumer finance industry since World War II has paralleled that of the consumer credit industry as a whole. The receivables of consumer finance companies expanded about three times during the 1950's and by an additional 50 per cent during the first five years in the 1960's. Their share of total instalment credit declined slightly during the 1950's but remained relatively constant at about 8.5 per cent in the early 1960's.

Within the consumer finance industry there has been a marked trend toward a growth in the size and importance of large companies. This study examines the changes in the financial positions of nine major companies.[1] All but one of these companies held more than $100 million in consumer receivables at the end of 1964 and all but one expanded more rapidly than the consumer credit industry as a whole during fifteen years from 1950 to 1964. Together they held 49 per cent of the receivables of all consumer-finance companies in 1955, 64 per cent in 1959, and 66 per cent by the end of 1964.

---

[1] This study is an extension for years 1960–64 of an earlier study by the author of these nine companies that was published in *Consumer Credit Costs, 1949–59*, Princeton, 1964. A description of the nature and composition of the sample and of procedures appears in Appendix 1.

The rapid expansion in the demand for consumer loans provided a favorable environment for their growth. Intense competition within the consumer finance industry and with institutions such as commercial banks, credit unions, and captive finance companies has, however, reduced the attractiveness and profitability of direct lending operations of this type. A number of changes in the environment in which they operate can be observed from changes in their financial statements: (1) There has been a gradual decline in the average gross income per $100 on consumer receivables throughout the entire period beginning in 1950 and ending in 1964. (2) There has been a decline in their operating expenses per $100 of receivables that paralleled approximately the decline in income. This trend was related in large part to an increase in the average size of loan, but it reflected the influence of many forces. (3) The net effects of the changes in earnings and expense rates led to a decline in the net operating return on consumer receivables. (4) Throughout the 1950's there was a general increase in interest rates and hence the cost of funds used in their lending operations. The average cost of borrowed funds reached a peak in 1960 and declined slightly in the early 1960's.

A number of changes in the operating procedures of these companies were probably stimulated at least in part by the changing competitive environment: (1) There was an increase in the proportion of income obtained from nonconsumer lending, insurance operations, and other nonlending activities. (2) They were able to use their resources more efficiently and reduced the proportion of their total assets held in cash and bank balances and other nonearning forms. (3) By increasing the ratio of debt to equity funds throughout most of the fifteen-year period, they were able to obtain somewhat greater financial leverage on borrowed funds.

On the average, these nine companies showed a slight decline in return on equity funds throughout the period as a whole, although there was considerable fluctuation from year to year. Net profits to equity funds averaged 11.9 per cent in the first five years of the sixties as compared with 12.8 per cent for the fifties as a whole. In addition to obtaining a somewhat smaller return on invested assets during the 1960's, the owners of these companies assumed greater risks in two forms: (1) by the exposure of their capital as indicated by the increase in the ratio of debt to equity funds, and (2) by placing their funds in higher risk loans as indicated by the increase in provisions for losses and actual losses in the recent years of the study.

Return on Consumer Receivables

The net operating income on consumer receivables as a percentage of the funds invested declined from $10.48 per $100 in the early part of the 1950's to $9.75 in the second five years, and finally to an average of $9.08 in the first five years of the 1960's. This decline reflected both a decrease in ratio of gross income to consumer receivables and an increase in operating expenses as a percentage of gross income (see Chart 4). The gross income of these nine companies declined by about $3 per $100 of receivables from the first half of the 1950's to the first half of the 1960's. During the same period, operating expenses as a percentage of gross income rose from 58.4 to 59.6 per cent and averaged about 60 per cent during 1962–64.

All but one of the nine companies reported a decrease in their gross income rate from 1960 to 1964, and all but two reported a decline in the rate of net operating income to receivables. One of these companies managed to reduce its operating expenses in relation to income and the other showed an improvement only because of an unusually large loss experience in 1960. The net operating return of the nine companies in 1964 varied from a low of $7.10 per $100 of consumer receivables to a high of $10.77 (see Chart 5). Expenses as a percentage of gross income ranged from 48 to 68 per cent. The company with the highest ratio of expenses to income also reported the highest gross income rate.

Gross Income on Consumer Receivables

The downward trend in gross income from funds invested in consumer receivables by consumer finance companies has been observed since the mid-thirties. The average gross income rate of two national companies declined from a high of $35 per hundred in 1933 to $21 per hundred at the end of 1964 (see Chart 6). Figures are not available for the nine-company sample for the thirties but the average gross income rate at these companies has declined from about $26 per hundred in the 1950's to $21.40 per hundred in 1964. In the last five years, the spread between the average received by all nine companies and that received by the two largest has decreased. In 1959 there was

CHART 4

Factors in Return on Consumer Receivables, 1950–64
(per $100 of average outstanding balances)

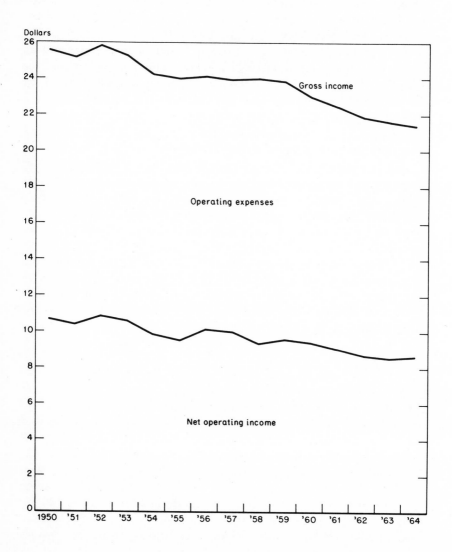

CHART 5

**Range of Return on Consumer Receivables
for Nine Companies, 1950–64
(net operating income per $100 of
average outstanding receivables)**

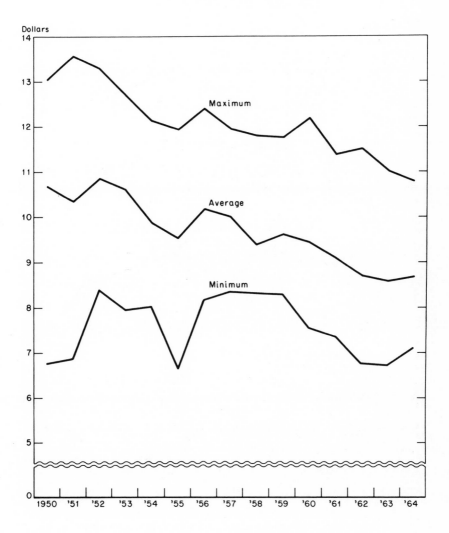

CHART 6

Gross Income from Consumer Receivables, 1930–41 and 1949–64
(per $100 of average outstanding balances)

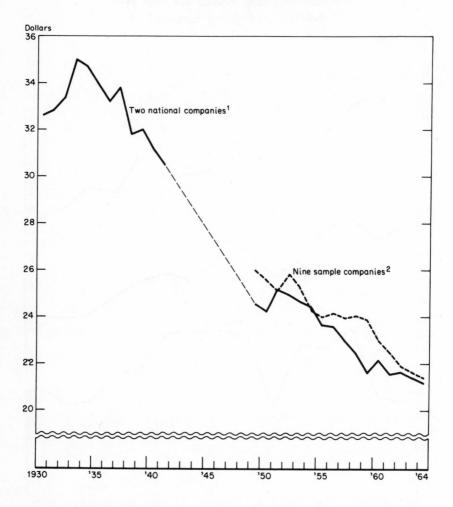

about a 2 percentage point spread between the two rates; by the end of 1964 there was less than a half percentage point difference.

There has been a slight reduction in the spread among the nine individual companies since the early 1950's, but the spread still ranges between six and seven percentage points. The highest rate reported by an individual company in 1964 was below the average for all companies in the early fifties. In recent years, six of the nine companies have been clustered within a range of two percentage points. The highest rate in 1964 was $24.50 per hundred and the lowest was $17.65 per hundred. The lowest rate, however, reflected the presence of a sizable amount of sales finance paper. The personal loan rate at the same company was $20.70 per hundred. The variations in rates on personal loans at all nine companies fell within a range of four percentage points.

One of the principal factors in the decline in the gross income rate on receivables has been the increase in average loan size, which, under the graduated ceiling rates, reduces the average finance charge. Data from the National Consumer Finance Association indicate that the average size of outstanding personal loans at consumer finance companies increased 2.7 times from the late 1930's to 1949, by another 70 per cent from 1949 to 1959, and by nearly 30 per cent in the first five years of the 1960's.[2] The raising of ceilings on loan size in some states and the introduction of new laws permitting large loans have contributed to an increase in the average size of loans at these companies and, in most cases, to a reduction in the average rate.

The average income rate at individual companies is also affected by the composition of their receivables. Personal lending under the small-loan laws or other cash lending laws dominates the activities of these companies. But most of them also engage to a lesser extent in the acquisition of sales finance paper on consumer goods of various types. The lender's gross income rate on these activities is normally somewhat below that on personal loans because of participation in the income by the dealer, rate concessions for bulk purchases, better collateral, or lower legal rates. The proportion of consumer receivables acquired indirectly (purchased from retailers) by these nine companies has not changed greatly, however, during the fifteen-year

[2] National Consumer Finance Association, *The Consumer Finance Industry*, Englewood Cliffs, N. J., Table 4–3, p. 59, gives the average unpaid balance on loans at consumer finance companies as $117 in 1939, $189 in 1949, and $326 in 1959. *NCFA Research Report on Finance Companies in 1964* gives a figure of $485 for 1964.

TABLE 4
Gross Income on Consumer Receivables, 1950–64
(dollars per $100 of outstanding balances)

	Gross Income on All Consumer Receivables	Gross Income on Personal Loans		
Date		Average Nine Companies	Highest	Lowest
1950–54 av.	25.20	27.00	33.20[a]	23.82[b]
1955–59 av.	23.99	25.20	29.20[c]	20.62[d]
1960	22.99	23.59	26.20	21.12
1961	22.48	22.94	25.00	20.87
1962	21.89	22.23	25.11	20.79
1963	21.63	21.97	24.55	21.01
1964	21.40	21.67	24.51	20.72

[a] Reported by one company in 1950.
[b] Reported by one company in 1950.
[c] Reported by one company in 1955.
[d] Reported by one company in 1959.

period covered by the study. Purchased receivables accounted for 9 per cent of total assets both at the beginning and end of the period covered, and fluctuated only slightly throughout. The proportion of receivables of this type, however, varies widely among the individual companies. Several companies held a negligible amount, and one company held about a fourth of its receivables in sales finance paper.

The average rates for personal loans are slightly above the average for all receivables but show the same general trends (see Table 4). The decline in the average rate on personal loans at all nine companies in the last five years seems to reflect in large part a reduction in the spread in the rates received by various companies rather than a decline in rates at all companies. The lowest rates have not shown any clear trend, but the highest rates declined in most recent years. The highest average rate on personal loans at any one company in the late 1950's was $29.20 per hundred and the lowest was $20.62. The highest average rate reported in 1964 was $24.51 per hundred and the lowest was $20.72 per hundred. In 1964 seven of the nine companies were within two percentage points of the lowest reported rate.

Operating Expenses

The operating expenses of the major consumer finance companies have been steadily declining from an average of $14.72 per hundred dollars in the first half of the 1950's to $14.24 in the second half and $13.16 in the first five years of the 1960's. The many factors affecting the costs of operation cannot be accurately identified or measured by the information available. Two counteracting forces, however, are known to have been operating that clearly played an important role in the changing pattern of expenses. First, wages and prices of most of the materials and services used by these companies have been increasing. Second, it is known that most costs are closely related to the number of accounts so that the increase in the average size of account has reduced the cost per dollar of handling each account.

In addition, several other forces may have served to reduce costs, but there is no way of determining how important they may have been. First, increases in the volume of business associated either with the general growth in demand for loans or, in particular, with the expansion in size of the nine companies included in this study may have introduced efficiencies of size. Second, improvement in managerial techniques, in particular the computerization of accounting and record keeping, may have reduced unit handling costs. Third, the legalization and growing use of precomputation of charges may have reduced computational costs.

All but one of the nine companies were able to reduce their operating expenses per $100 of receivables during the first half of the 1960's. Five of these were able to reduce their expenses by more than the decline in gross income. Operating expenses as a percentage of gross income increased from 59 to 60 per cent from 1960 to 1964. The ratio of operating expenses to income ranged from 48 to 68 per cent in 1964. In one case, expenses increased as a percentage of income from 63 to 68 per cent in the early sixties.

Despite advancing wage rates, salaries and related personnel costs declined per hundred dollars of receivables in a gradual but steady trend throughout the fifteen-year period from 1950 to 1964 (see Table 5). Salary costs, which amounted to $6.75 per $100 of receivables in the early 1950's, decreased to $6.00 in the early 1960's and to a low of $5.60 in 1964. Eight companies showed some decline during the early 1960's, and salary costs in 1964 ranged between a low of $4.48 per hundred dollars of receivables and a high of $6.67 (Table 6).

Occupancy costs, which include rent and the service costs of maintaining office space, have decreased only slightly during the last fifteen years. The reported costs of occupancy varied widely among the nine companies and ranged from $.71 to $1.13 per hundred of receivables in 1964.

TABLE 5

Components of Finance Charges on Consumer Receivables, 1950–64

(dollars per $100 of average outstanding credit)

Item	Averages		1960	1961	1962	1963	1964
	1950–54	1955–59					
Lender's income (finance charges after deduction of dealer's share)[a]	25.20	23.99	22.99	22.48	21.89	21.63	21.40
Operating expenses, total	14.72	14.24	13.53	13.38	13.17	13.03	12.73
Salaries	6.75	6.53	6.07	6.00	5.90	5.77	5.60
Occupancy costs	1.07	1.06	1.03	1.02	1.02	.98	.98
Advertising	1.10	.88	.82	.75	.73	.75	.71
Provisions for losses	1.89	1.85	2.28	2.22	2.33	2.33	2.27
Other	3.89	3.90	3.30	3.37	3.18	3.19	3.18
Nonoperating expenses, total (net operating income)	10.48	9.75	9.44	9.10	8.70	8.58	8.67
Cost of nonequity funds	2.70	3.58	4.29	4.12	4.10	4.11	4.17
Income taxes	3.84	2.96	2.60	2.39	2.23	2.16	2.17
Cost of equity funds (lender's profit)	3.94	3.20	2.56	2.59	2.36	2.31	2.33
Retained	1.00	.73	.67	.79	.72	.83	.79
Dividends	2.94	2.47	1.80	1.80	1.63	1.47	1.53

Note: Data may not add to totals because of rounding.

[a] The lender's gross income excludes a small amount of the gross finance charge to consumers that is shared with the dealer on contracts purchased from dealers. In 1950 this figure was estimated to be only 17 cents per $100 of loans.

TABLE 6

Range in Operating Expenses by Type of Expense, 1964

(dollars per $100 of average outstanding credit)

Item	Nine-Company Average	Range of Ratios (dollars)[a]	
		Highest	Lowest
Operating expenses, total	12.73	16.39	9.99
Salaries	5.60	6.67	4.48
Occupancy costs	.98	1.13	.71
Advertising	.71	1.55	.13
Provisions for losses	2.27	2.90	1.51
Other	3.18	4.80	2.11

[a] Components in columns for highest and lowest ratios are not additive, as ratios were taken from statements for different companies.

TABLE 7
Provisions for Losses and Actual Losses, 1950–64
(per $100 of average outstanding receivables)

Date	Provisions for Losses	Actual Losses (net charge-offs)		
		Average	Highest	Lowest
1950–54 av.	1.89	1.44	3.01[a]	.51[b]
1955–59 av.	1.85	1.46	2.78[c]	.45[d]
1960	2.28	1.75	2.39	.98
1961	2.22	1.91	2.97	1.29
1962	2.33	1.90	2.84	1.03
1963	2.33	1.93	2.55	1.18
1964	2.27	1.93	2.38	1.14

[a] Reported by one company in 1951.
[b] Reported by one company in 1951.
[c] Reported by one company in 1958.
[d] Reported by one company in 1956.

Advertising costs showed the sharpest decline of any identifiable item of expense. Expenditure for advertising and promotion dropped from a high of $1.25 per hundred dollars of receivables in 1950 to $.71 in 1964. A downward trend was observed in all but one company in the early 1960's. The range in expenditures for advertising was the largest of all expense items and varied from a low of $.13 per hundred dollars of receivables to a high of $1.55.

Only one of the major expense items, provisions for losses, did not decline during the period covered by the study. During the 1950's the provisions varied somewhat from year to year without any recognizable trend. In 1958 they increased to about $2 per $100 of receivables and in 1960 they increased again to $2.28 and remained at about that level in subsequent years (see Table 7). Actual losses, as measured by gross charge-offs net of recoveries, followed the same general pattern but at a slightly lower level. Net charge-offs averaged $1.44 per $100 of receivables in the first half of the 1950's. This level rose to about $1.70 in the years 1958 to 1960 and then to about $1.90 in the last four years of the study. Individual company losses in 1964 ranged from $1.14 to $2.38 per $100 of receivables. A comparison of company growth rates and changes in net charge-offs from 1960 to 1964 does not show any apparent relationship between company expansion and the losses incurred. Three of the four companies that had the most rapid growth reported a slight decline in their net charge-offs during that period.

TABLE 8

Distribution of Operating Expenses on Consumer Receivables
by Type of Expense, 1950–64

(per cent)

Item	Averages		1960	1961	1962	1963	1964
	1950–54	1955–59					
Operating expenses, total	100.0	100.0	100.0	100.0	100.0	100.0	100.0
Salaries	45.9	45.9	44.9	44.9	44.8	44.3	44.0
Occupancy costs	7.2	7.5	7.8	7.7	7.7	7.5	7.7
Advertising	7.7	6.2	6.1	5.6	5.6	5.8	5.6
Provisions for losses	12.8	13.0	16.8	16.6	17.7	17.9	17.8
Other	26.4	27.4	24.4	25.2	24.2	24.5	24.9

The distribution of operating expenses by type, as shown in Table 8, points up even more vividly the shift in expenses that has been taking place. Salaries and advertising expenses have both decreased in importance by about two percentage points from the early 1950's to the early 1960's. Occupancy costs were in general somewhat higher than in the 1950's. Miscellaneous expenses increased in importance in the late 1950's and then in the 1960's dropped back to a level a point or two below that of the early 1950's. Only provisions for losses showed any substantial increase in importance.

The role of salaries varied from 42 to 48 per cent of total operating expenses among the nine companies in 1964. All but three of them reported some reduction in the importance of this item. Advertising costs, which varied from 1 to 10 per cent of the total among the different companies, declined at all but one company during the 1960's. Occupancy costs, which ranged from about 5 to 11 per cent of expenses, fell at five of the nine companies. Provisions for losses increased at all but three companies and in one of these cases an unusually large loss in the early 1960's distorted the comparison. Provision for losses ranged from 15 to 20 per cent of total operating expenses at various companies in 1964 and was second only to salaries as a separate item of operating expense.

The increase in provision for losses during the early 1960's was the most distinctive shift in the pattern of expenses. With provision for losses increasing by more than a third over the average for 1950, this element of expense alone was large enough to account for the decline in return on consumer receivables. Since the added cost of handling risky loans includes many types of expenses in addition to provisions for losses, it seems likely that added risks have played an important role in the reduced profitability of consumer lending operations. This change may have been necessitated by the competitive environment and may have been required to maintain a large enough volume for efficient operations. It does not necesarily follow that the return on consumer receivables would have been higher if the additional risks had not been taken.

Nonoperating Expenses

The lender's view of costs is sometimes limited to what has been referred to as operating costs plus the cost of borrowed money and taxes. The economist, however, views costs as including "normal profits," defined as the return on capital that is essential to the retention of funds in the industry. Under competitive conditions and free entry into the industry, larger than normal profits attract new funds and less than normal profits lead to the withdrawal of funds. For purposes of this study the return to the owners is included in nonoperating expenses and is discussed separately. Nonoperating expenses—defined to include the cost of nonequity funds, income taxes, and the cost of equity or the lender's profit—are shown in Table 5.

Nonoperating expenses have decreased gradually in recent years, and the total of $8.67 per $100 of receivables in 1964 was nearly $2.00 below the average for the first half of the 1950's. The decline reflected a gradually downward trend in both the cost of equity funds and income tax payments. Part of the recent decline in income tax expenses can be traced to changes in corporate tax rates.

The pronounced upward trend in the cost of nonequity funds that prevailed during the 1950's ended with a peak in 1960. During the years 1961 to 1964, the costs remained relatively stable at an average of $4.12 per $100 of receivables.

Related Earning Activities

Throughout the years covered by the study, these companies have increased their activities in business areas other than lending to consumers. Their investment in nonconsumer earning assets averaged

TABLE 9

Comparison of Net Operating Income from Consumer Receivables
and from Other Sources, 1950–64

(per cent)

| | | | Net Operating Income | | |
| | Distribution of Net Operating Income from | | From Consumer Receivables to Outstanding Receivables | From All Sources to Earning Assets | Column 4 Minus Column 3 |
Year	Consumer Receivables (1)	Other Sources (2)	(3)	(4)	(5)
1950–54 av.	93.4	6.6	10.5	11.0	0.5
1955–59 av.	91.9	8.1	9.7	10.5	0.8
1960	90.6	9.4	9.4	10.2	0.8
1961	88.8	11.2	9.1	10.0	0.9
1962	85.3	14.7	8.7	9.8	1.1
1963	84.6	15.4	8.7	9.7	1.0
1964	84.2	15.8	8.7	9.6	0.9

TABLE 10

Distribution of Assets, End of Year, 1950–64

(per cent)

| | Averages | | | | | | |
Item	1950–54	1955–59	1960	1961	1962	1963	1964
Earning assets, net	85.0	86.6	88.6	88.6	89.3	90.4	90.9
Consumer credit	83.3	85.4	86.2	86.0	85.0	84.7	84.5
Personal loans	73.7	76.6	76.4	76.9	76.3	76.3	75.6
Other	9.6	8.8	9.8	9.1	8.7	8.4	8.9
Nonconsumer	1.7	1.2	2.4	2.6	4.3	5.7	6.4
Cash and bank balances	11.5	9.8	8.3	8.0	7.7	6.8	6.2
Other assets	3.5	3.6	3.1	3.4	3.0	2.8	2.9
Total	100.0	100.0	100.0	100.0	100.0	100.0	100.0

about 1.5 per cent of total assets throughout the 1950's. This figure
had doubled by 1960, and increased to 6.4 per cent of the total by the
end of 1964 (see Table 10). This trend can be observed even more
clearly in the proportion of net operating income received from insurance and nonconsumer activities. The ratio of net operating income
from these miscellaneous activities to the total averaged 7.5 per cent

throughout the 1950's (see Table 9). In 1960 this ratio increased to 9.4 per cent and it reached 15.8 per cent by 1964. The importance of income from insurance and nonconsumer activities may be somewhat exaggerated by these figures because of accounting difficulties involved in segregating expenses on joint activities that are frequently conducted by the same personnel and with the same facilities. But any bias in the level does not alter the value of these figures as evidence of an increasing attention to business activities other than direct lending to consumers.

Insurance operations provided an additional source of income for all of the companies, but some of them also engaged in business lending and other types of business activities. The participation of the nine companies in outside activities ranged widely from one company that reported only 1.3 per cent of its net operating income from nonconsumer sources to another that reported 28 per cent from such sources.

Effective Use of Total Resources

All business operations tie up some funds in bank balances and non-earning assets that could be used to produce income. The costs of these funds are directly related to the amounts involved. In the early 1950's the sample companies held 15 per cent of their total assets in nonearning forms. This percentage was reduced slightly in the last part of the 1950's and has been reduced even more in recent years. By the end of 1964 the proportion of nonearning assets to total assets dropped to 9.1 per cent (see last two items in Table 10).

The principal reduction was made in cash and bank balances, which had amounted to about 12 per cent of assets during the early 1950's. This figure dropped to 8 per cent in 1960 and to 6.2 per cent by the end of 1964. Some of the improvement may reflect the more efficient management of cash balances, but, more importantly, it also reflects a reduction in the amounts held in compensating balances with banks.

The reduction in bank balances accompanied the decline in bank borrowing as a source of short-term funds. In the early 1950's banks provided more than a third of the total resources of the nine major companies. This percentage dropped to 18.5 per cent in 1960 and was at a low of 17.9 per cent at the end of 1964. The shift was made possible by the generally favorable conditions in the credit market and by the availability of alternative sources of funds (see Table 11).

TABLE 12
Distribution of Nine Companies by Ratio of Net Operating Income
to Total Assets, 1960 and 1964

Net Operating Income to Total Assets (per cent)	1960	1964
10.0–11.3	2	3
9.0–9.9	2	—
8.0–8.9	4	2
7.0–7.9	1	4
Nine-company average	9.0	8.7

TABLE 13
Factors Affecting Return on Total Assets, 1960–64
(increasing +, decreasing −)

Factor	Average All Companies	Individual Companies								
		1	2	3	4	5	6	7	8	9
Increase in gross income rate on consumer receivables (+)	−	−	−	+	−	−	−	−	−	−
Decrease in operating expenses as percentage of income (+)	−	+	+	+	−	−	−	+	+	−
Decrease in operating expenses exclusive of provision for losses as percentage of income (+)	+	−	+	−	+	+	−	+	+	−
Decrease in provision for losses as percentage of income (+)	−	+	−	+	−	−	−	−	−	−
Increase in proportion of net operating income from non-credit activities (+)	+	+	+	−	+	+	+	+	−	+
Decrease in nonearning assets as percentage of total assets (+)	+	+	+	+	+	+	+	+	+	−
Change in return on total assets (+)	−	+	−	−	−	−	−	+	+	−

portion of their net operating income obtained from nonconsumer sources. In both of the exceptional cases, the decline in income from these sources was very small and did not represent a major factor affecting their returns. (5) All but one company reduced the proportion of assets held in nonearning forms.

TABLE 14
Cost of Nonequity Funds, 1950–64
(percentage of average outstanding balances)

| Date | Debt | Ratio of Dollar Costs of Nonequity Funds to | |
		Total Nonequity Funds	Nonequity Funds Minus Nonearning Assests
1950–54 av.	3.5	3.2	4.1
1955–59 av.	4.4	4.1	5.3
1960	5.3	5.0	5.9
1961	5.1	4.8	5.7
1962	5.1	4.8	5.6
1963	5.1	4.8	5.5
1964	5.2	4.8	5.5

Role of Financing in Profits

Favorable conditions in the credit markets during the early 1960's contributed to the profitable operations of these companies in two ways: (1) they were able to reduce the average rate paid for funds slightly; (2) they were able to increase the financial advantage of using borrowed funds by increasing the ratio of nonequity to equity funds.

The cost of nonequity funds as measured by the ratio of the total cost of borrowed funds to the average balances of nonequity funds declined from a high of 5.0 per cent in 1960 to 4.8 per cent the following four years. This easing of the average rate paid for funds gave these companies relief from the steady upward trend in money costs that prevailed throughout most of the 1950's.

In addition to the easing of interest rates, credit conditions made possible a further reduction in money costs by permitting them to shift to sources that do not require compensating balances (see Table 11). As has previously been indicated, this study has treated the cost of compensating balances as a reduction in the earning power of assets rather than as a factor increasing the effective rate on borrowed funds. If nonearning assets are subtracted from nonequity funds in computing the rate on nonequity funds, the decline in the net money costs from 1960 to 1964 was nearly a half a percentage point (see Table 14).

The pattern of interest costs at various companies differed somewhat, and four of the companies paid slightly more for the nonequity

TABLE 15
Role of Nonequity Funds in Profits, 1950–64
(per cent)

Item	Averages		1960	1961	1962	1963	1964
	1950–54	1955–59					
1. Profits before taxes to equity funds	24.6	23.8	21.6	21.2	20.9	21.6	21.7
2. Net operating income to total assets	9.4	9.1	9.0	8.9	8.7	8.7	8.7
3. Return added on equity by use of nonequity funds (line 1 minus line 2, or line 5 times line 6)[a]	15.2	14.7	12.6	12.3	12.2	12.9	13.0
4. Cost of nonequity funds	3.2	4.1	5.0	4.8	4.8	4.8	4.8
5. Net return on nonequity funds (line 2 minus line 4)	6.2	5.0	4.0	4.1	3.9	3.9	3.9
6. Ratio, nonequity to equity funds	2.5	3.0	3.3	3.2	3.3	3.5	3.6
7. Percentage of profits obtained from leverage on nonequity funds (line 3 divided by line 1)	61.8	61.8	58.3	58.0	58.4	59.7	59.9

[a] The two methods of calculation do not produce exactly the same results on the basis of data in this table because of differences introduced by rounding and averaging procedures.

funds in 1964 than in 1960. The differences, however, were very small. The major declines occurred at the companies that had paid the highest rates in 1960.

In addition to the slight decline in the cost of borrowed money, the sample companies obtained a further financial advantage by increasing the ratio of nonequity to equity funds. This ratio rose to 3.6 in 1964 as compared to 3.3 in 1960 and 2.4 in 1950. The advantage for consumer finance companies in borrowing money lies in their ability to earn more on the funds than they pay for them. Since the ratio of net operating income to total assets is a measure of the average earnings on each dollar of assets, the company must obtain funds at a rate below the return on assets if they are to use debt profitably. The spread between the return on assets and cost of nonequity funds has. been gradually declining during the fifteen years from 1950 to 1964 (see Table 15, line 5). In the 1950's the decline resulted primarily from the increase in the cost of funds and in the early 1960's from the decline in the return on assets. The net return on nonequity funds varied widely in 1964 for the individual companies, from a low of 2.3

to a high of 6 percentage points, reflecting both variations in the return on assets and in the rate paid for borrowed funds.

The contribution of debt to the owner's income increases with the ratio of debt to equity, so that the return to owners from the use of debt can be obtained by multiplying the net return on nonequity funds by the ratio of nonequity to equity funds. For all nine companies the ratio of debt to equity in 1964 was 3.6, up from 3.3 in 1960 and from 2.4 in 1950. The use of debt added about thirteen percentage points to the return to the owners in 1964, which together with a return on assets of 8.7 per cent, brought the return on equity before taxes to 21.7 per cent (see Table 15).

The leverage ratio or ratio of nonequity to equity funds for individual companies in 1964 varied from 2.1 to 5.1 and, when multiplied by the net return on debt, gave the owners a profit from the use of debt ranging from 10.9 to 19.6 percentage points. The variation in range of the contribution of debt to profits at individual companies was smaller than the variation in the net return on debt. In general the companies with low returns on debt showed a higher ratio of nonequity to equity funds.

During the 1950's the effects of increases in interest cost on profits were offset in large part by increases in the ratio of nonequity to equity funds. If the nonequity to equity funds ratio for the early 1950's were applied to the 1964 earnings and cost data, the average rate of profit before taxes to equity would be only half the rate that prevailed in 1964. The expansion of debt financing has played a critical role in the maintenance of the industry's profits over the last fifteen years. The increase in debt in relation to equity, however, also increased the risk exposure of the owners.

Profits

Profits before taxes at the sample companies have remained relatively stable at about 21 to 22 per cent of equity since 1958 (see Table 16). This is down from an average of 24.6 per cent in the early 1950's. Reductions in income tax rates have permitted somewhat smaller provisions for taxes in recent years and have reduced the effects of adverse factors on the profit rate to some extent. Net profits were 12.2 per cent of equity funds in 1964, which was sightly below the average for most of the 1950's but above the first few years of the 1960's. Although these consumer finance companies have been able to main-

TABLE 16
Consumer Finance Company Profits, 1950–64
(per cent)

Date	Profits Before Taxes to Equity Funds	Provisions for Income Taxes to Profit Before Taxes	Net Profits to Equity Funds	Range-Net Profit Rate	
				Highest	Lowest
1950–54 av.	24.6	48.4	12.7	17.7[a]	8.0[b]
1955–59 av.	23.8	45.8	12.9	19.9[c]	8.1[d]
1960	21.6	47.1	11.4	13.6	5.8
1961	21.2	44.3	11.8	15.8	8.0
1962	20.9	43.4	11.8	15.2	7.8
1963	21.6	42.7	12.3	16.5	10.1
1964	21.7	43.6	12.2	16.2	9.4

[a] Reported by one company in 1950.
[b] Reported by one company in 1950.
[c] Reported by one company in 1955.
[d] Reported by one company in 1955.

tain a relatively stable profit rate throughout the period covered, this stability has been achieved at the expense of somewhat greater risk during a period when rates of return on investment in other types of enterprise have been moving upward.

Although the average profit rate for all nine companies increased slightly from 1960 to 1964, only four out of the nine companies reported a higher rate. Table 17 shows the range of variations among individual companies and indicates that lower taxes, lower money costs, and higher debt-equity ratios were favorable at most companies, but in most cases these factors were not large enough to offset the decline in the return on total assets.

Comparison of Companies with Highest and Lowest Charges to Consumers

The spread between companies with highest and lowest charge in 1964 was about seven percentage points, with the highest obtaining an average gross income of $24.51 per hundred dollars of receivables and the lowest obtaining an income of $17.65. Since the income con-

TABLE 17
Factors Affecting Return of Equity, 1960–64
(increasing, +; decreasing, −)

Factor	Average All Com- panies	Individual Companies								
		1	2	3	4	5	6	7	8	9
Increase in return on total assets (+)	−	+	−	−	−	−	−	−	+	+	−
Decrease in rate paid on nonequity funds (+)	+	−	+	+	−	+	+	+	−	−	
Increase in ratio of debt to equity (+)	+	+	+	+	+	+	+	+	+	−	
Decrease in provision for income taxes (+)	+	+	+	+	−	+	+	−	+	+	
Change in rate of return after taxes on equity funds (+)	+	+	+	−	−	−	−	+	+	−	

sists of charges to consumer for the outstanding balances, these rates also measure the average finance charge paid by the consumer to the company. They exclude, however, any participation by dealers in the charge, but in the case of these companies such amounts would be very small.

Several of the nine companies were consistently reported to have the highest charge and several reported the lowest. The financial ratios for these companies were averaged for the five-year period 1960–64, and are shown as "high- and low-charge" companies in Table 18.

The two companies with the highest charges showed an average gross income of $24.80 per $100 of receivables, $4.26 higher than the average for the two companies with the lowest charges. The high-charge companies also had the highest operating costs, so that the higher earning rates were largely offset by higher costs. The ratios of net operating income to consumer receivables at the two groups of companies were almost identical.

All items of expense except occupancy costs were higher at the high-charge companies. Provision for losses at the high-charge companies were about a third higher, which suggests that a part of the cost difference may have reflected cost associated with riskier loans. Advertising costs at the high-charge companies were nearly double those at the companies with lower charges.

TABLE 18

Comparison of Companies with Highest and Lowest Average
Finance Charges, 1960–64

Item	Two High-Charge Companies (1)	Two Low-Charge Companies (2)	Difference (col. 1 minus col. 2) (3)
Dollars per $100 of Average Outstanding Consumer Receivables			
Finance charges[a]	24.80	20.54	4.26
Operating expenses	15.69	11.38	4.31
Salaries	6.74	5.06	1.68
Occupancy costs	.89	1.14	− .25
Advertising	1.17	.68	.49
Provisions for losses	2.62	1.98	.64
Other	4.27	2.52	1.75
Net operating income	9.11	9.16	− .05
Selected Ratios (per cent)			
Total net operating income to earning assets	9.5	9.6	−0.1
Total net operating income to total assets	8.3	8.5	−0.2
Cost of nonequity funds	4.9	4.6	0.3
Nonequity to equity funds (ratio)	3.3	3.1	0.2
Net profit to equity funds	11.2	10.5	0.7

Note: All data are averages of annual individual company ratios for five years,
1960–64.

[a] Excludes dealer share of gross finance charge.

Comparison of Companies with Highest and Lowest Profit Rates

Data for two of the companies that were generally shown to have the highest return on equity and two that generally showed the lowest return on equity are compared in Table 19. Quite surprisingly, the difference in operating income and expense on consumer receivables differs only slightly, with the high-profit companies reporting a slightly lower net operating income on consumer receivables than the less profitable companies.

The major source of extra profit for the profitable companies appeared to be in their insurance and nonconsumer activities. The two profitable companies showed a net operating income on all earning assets that was 1.4 percentage points higher than that of the less profit-

TABLE 19
Comparison of Selected High- and Low-Profit Companies, 1960–64

Item	Two High-Profit Companies (1)	Two Low-Profit Companies (2)	Difference (col. 1 minus col. 2) (3)
Selected Ratios (per cent)			
Net profit to equity funds	14.4	10.2	4.2
Net operating income on consumer receivables to average receivables	8.5	8.6	−0.1
Total net operating income:			
to earning assets	10.8	9.4	1.4
to total assets	9.4	8.0	1.4
Cost of nonequity funds	4.9	5.1	−0.2
Nonequity to equity funds (ratio)	3.6	3.7	−0.1
Dollars per $100 of Average Outstanding Consumer Receivables			
Finance charges[a]	22.45	22.06	.39
Operating expenses	13.96	13.49	.47
Salaries	5.94	6.18	−.24
Occupancy costs	1.24	.69	.55
Advertising	.79	1.05	−.26
Provisions for losses	2.45	2.23	.22
Other	3.52	3.33	.19
Net operating income	8.49	8.58	−.09

Note: All data are averages of individual company ratios for five years, 1960–64.
[a] Excludes dealer share of gross finance charge.

able firms. This rate was carried into a higher return on total assets which, when multiplied by the leverage of debt operations, resulted in a 4.2 per cent higher return on equity at the high-profit companies. The high-profit companies had a fractionally lower interest cost, but this was offset in part by a lower leverage ratio so that the only distinct advantage for the profitable companies was in their earnings on nonlending activities.

The results of this comparison contrast sharply with a study of high-profit companies in the same sample for the 1950's.[3] In the earlier study, part of the higher return could be traced to more profitable consumer lending activities as well as to nonconsumer activities.

[3] See Smith, *Consumer Credit Costs*, p. 27.

III

A Cross-Section Study of Industry
Costs and Earnings

JACK ZWICK

*Graduate School of Business,
Columbia University*

The preceding chapter examined trends in costs and earnings incurred by nine large consumer finance companies between 1949 and 1964. The analysis is extended here to examine the structural characteristics of a larger sample of consumer finance companies during a three-year period (1962–64). The objective of this chapter is to ascertain how operating costs and earnings per $100 of loans outstanding differ according to various characteristics of forty-eight companies. More precisely, the purpose is to analyze in detail the factors which appear to influence the costs and profits of making small loans. A summary of the findings is presented prior to a detailed description of the research method, the data examined, and evidence supporting the findings.

Summary of Findings

Although numerous factors have a bearing on the costs associated with making small loans, statistical analysis suggests that some are substantially more important than others. More specifically, the size of the average loan which a company makes; the characteristic division in company lending among business loans, sales finance loans, and cash

55

loans to consumers; and the degree of credit risk which the firm typically assumes appear to influence lending costs most significantly. The smaller the average loan size, the higher the costs. Similarly, the larger the proportion of consumer cash loans in a company's loan portfolio, the higher the costs. Also, as one would expect, the more risky the loan portfolio, the higher the costs.

At the same time, these company characteristics have a similar relationship to gross income. For example, the smaller the average loan size, the higher the gross income. Again, the larger the proportion of consumer cash loans, the higher the gross income. And finally, the more risky the loan portfolio, the higher the gross income. Thus there is a distinct tendency for both higher costs and higher gross income (or lower costs and lower gross income) to be associated with different average loan sizes, different proportions of cash loans in the loan mix, and different degrees of loan risk observed in the sample companies. Quite interestingly, the cost and the gross income differences associated with these company characteristics are largely offsetting, and as a consequence operating profits (gross income minus operating costs) are not materially affected.

What variables, then, appear to account for differences in operating profits? The degree of loan office utilization—i.e., the number of loans which a company makes divided by the number of offices—is such a variable. Companies which make comparatively larger numbers of loans per average office are more profitable and, as the analysis also indicates, there is a significant tendency for large companies to achieve higher degrees of loan office utilization.

These conclusions may have important implications for both firms in the consumer finance industry and the regulatory authorities. At the level of the firm the implicit recommendation is that firms should pursue strategies enabling them to achieve higher levels of loan office utilization. The findings imply that improvement in the direction of loan office utilization will benefit operating profits more than changes in other company characteristics. The findings also have interesting implications for the regulatory authorities, although the available data cannot fully substantiate these implications. They suggest that differences in loan ceilings and rate structures established by the authorities in the various states do not significantly affect the profitability of operations; this is due to the compensating effects of operating costs and gross income in relation to differences in the average size of loans outstanding. In effect, to the extent that variations in average loan size, loan risk, and loan mix result in revenue and cost differences

TABLE 20

Average Loan Size, Number of Loans Outstanding per Office, and Total Costs
per $100 of Loans Outstanding

Company	Total Costs per $100 of Loans Outstanding	No. of Loans Outstanding per Office	Average Loan Size
1	$18.90	408	$480
2	17.70	476	472
3	22.90	523	395
4	18.40	597	372
5	19.30	675	598
6	21.80	789	434
7	25.30	842	223
8	19.30	901	361
9	22.10	1033	396
10	20.00	1226	342

which cancel out, the existing rate structures provide fairly similar
rates of operating profit. On the other hand, regulatory limitations on
the number of offices in a state may indirectly enhance profitability
of operations (profits per dollar of loans) to the extent that the
limitations result in higher numbers of loans per office.

The Research Method

The multiple regression technique is used to identify company characteristics related to costs and earnings net of the influence of other
company characteristics. This statistical technique is frequently employed when it is desirable to isolate the relation between two or more
independent variables with respect to a third, dependent variable.
Table 20 contains data for ten consumer finance companies regarding
costs per $100 of loans outstanding, number of loans outstanding per
loan office, and average loan size. The objective is to separate the relation between costs and the number of loans per office from the relation between costs and average loan size.

The data of Table 20 suggest that costs per $100 of loans outstand-
ing tend to be higher for companies making relatively large numbers
of loans per office. This inference is supported visually in Chart 7,
based on Table 20, where costs and loans per office are summarized for
each company as plotted points. A "least squares" line fitted to the
plotted points in the chart (the solid line) has an upward slope, sug-

CHART 7

Costs and Loans per Office

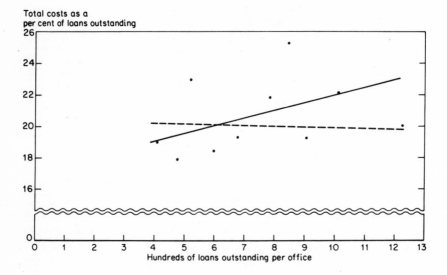

Total costs as a
per cent of loans outstanding

Hundreds of loans outstanding per office

gesting that costs increase as the number of loans outstanding per office increases.

In point of fact, the impression conveyed by the data that costs rise among the ten companies as the number of loans per office increases is probably misleading. The costs for the ten companies shown in the table actually vary inversely with average loan size. The companies making smaller average-size loans incur higher costs and, at the same time, make larger numbers of loans per office. Thus costs per $100 of loans appear to rise as the number of loans per office increases. But what would be the relation between the number of loans per office and costs if differences in average loan size were not present?

It is possible by use of the multiple regression technique to separate the relation between costs and average loan size from the relation between costs and number of loans per office. In Chart 7 a dotted line is drawn which suggests the average relation between costs and number of loans per office after the relation between costs and different average loan sizes for the ten companies has been eliminated. This moderately downward-sloping line, which is obtained when the multiple regression technique is applied to the variables given in the following section, suggests that more loans outstanding per office may be accompanied by slightly lower costs per $100 of outstandings, holding average loan size constant.[1] Thus the multiple regression technique suggests an important finding regarding cost characteristics—i.e., costs per $100 of outstandings are not necessarily higher for companies making more loans per office when average loan size is held constant. This inference was not apparent from inspection of the basic data in Table 20.[2]

The Sample and the Data

Using the multiple regression technique, data have been analyzed for a sample comprised of forty-eight consumer finance companies which responded to the National Consumer Finance Association's (NCFA) annual questionnaires. In recent years, member companies of the NCFA which operate five or more loan offices have been requested to complete detailed questionnaires concerning their operating and financial characteristics. The analysis of factors affecting costs and earnings is applied to the data of forty-eight of these companies which responded in sufficient detail to the NCFA questionnaires concerning their operations from 1962 through 1964.[3] These forty-eight

[1] A definite conclusion cannot be reached since the multiple regression result for the ten companies is not statistically significant.

[2] The multiple regression result is meaningful only when the independent variables are truly independent of one another and when statistical tests confirm that the result is not likely to have occurred by chance.

[3] For purposes of the cross-section analysis it was considered desirable to examine more than one year's results, and data for the years 1962–64 were collected and synthesized. Only companies which responded to the NCFA questionnaires in each of the three years were included. There were fifty-three companies; of them, five respondents in at least one of the three years failed to supply data concerning one of the variables included in the study. It was therefore necessary to discard the data for these five companies. The remaining forty-eight companies fall into the following six size categories:

Asset Size in Millions of Dollars (1962–64)	Number of Companies
Above 500	2
150–500	6
50–150	4
10–50	12
5–10	13
1–5	11

companies held $4,720 million of instalment credit, or 93 per cent of the $5,078 million of consumer finance instalment credit reported outstanding at the end of 1964 by the Federal Reserve Board.

The NCFA questionnaires obtained from each of the forty-eight companies data regarding costs, earnings, company size, important asset and liability characteristics, and various other items considered useful in studying the determinants of costs and profitability. The characteristics concerning each company which have been gathered and analyzed are listed below:

1. Cost variables expressed as a percentage of loans outstanding at year end:

Total operating costs (Y_1)[4]
Operating cost components
  Wage and salary expenses (Y_4)
  Advertising expenses
  Losses
  Other operating expenses (Y_5)

2. Earnings variables expressed as a percentage of loans outstanding at year end:

Gross income (Y_2)
Operating income before interest and taxes (EBIT) (Y_3)[5]

3. Miscellaneous other variables:

Average loan size (X_1)—personal loans outstanding at year end—divided by the number of personal loans outstanding at year end
Loan risk (X_2)—net charge-offs (losses net of recoveries) as a percentage of average loans outstanding
Loan mix (X_3)—sales finance and business loans as a percentage of loans outstanding at year end
Number of loans outstanding per office (X_4)—number of loans outstanding at year end per loan office

---

A large proportion of small loan companies—those operating fewer than five offices—were excluded from the analysis due to data limitations. Thus, the findings apply to the larger companies, even though there is wide variation in size among the sample companies.

[4] The symbols Y_1, X_4, etc., serve to identify the different variables as they appear in the multiple regression tests. The Y's are dependent variables and the X's are independent variables in the various tests.

[5] $Y_3 = Y_2 - Y_1$.

Loan-to-asset ratio (X_5)—total loans at year end as a percentage of total assets at year end

Company size (X_6)—the log of total assets at year end

New-borrower ratio (X_7)—number of personal loans to new borrowers divided by the number of personal loans outstanding at year end

Each company's responses to the NCFA questionnaires in 1962, 1963, and 1964 were used to compute the variables shown. Each year's figures were first analyzed separately before averaging them for the three years. The 1962–64 average figures have been used in the analysis and exposition which follows. (It should be noted, however, that the statistical results based on the figures for the three individual years do not differ appreciably from the results based on 1962–64 average data.)[6]

As indicated above, operating costs and gross income are both expressed per $100 dollars of total loans outstanding.[7] This method of expressing costs and revenues is similar but not identical to that used in Chapter II.[8] These cost-loan and income-loan measures are derived by dividing total loans outstanding for each sample company into operating costs and income respectively, and by multiplying the quotient by 100.

Factors Affecting Operating Costs

It was originally presumed that differences in operating cost ratios (operating costs per $100 of loans outstanding) could best be ex-

[6] If exposition had been based on the results obtained in a single year, the possibility exists that unusual economic conditions or accounting practices in that year might have affected to some extent the relation between the structural characteristics of the sample companies and their costs and earnings. When the data for three years are averaged together, the likelihood of distortions due to unusual factors affecting a single year's data is substantially reduced. Also, one important variable included in the analysis—the ratio of net charge-offs to loans outstanding—has limited economic meaning when computed for a single year. (Charge-offs in a given year are largely related to loans made during previous years.) Averaging both charge-offs and average outstandings for three years reduces substantially the distortion occasioned by using a single year's figures to study the lagged relationship between these two variables.

[7] "Loans outstanding" are defined as gross outstandings less loss reserves and less unearned income.

[8] In the preceding chapter and in his earlier book, Paul F. Smith expressed income and expenses as percentages of the average of beginning- and end-of-year consumer receivables. See *Consumer Credit Costs, 1949–1959*, New York, 1964.

plained in terms of seven company characteristics inherent in the data. First, operating costs among the forty-eight companies were expected to decline with increasing average loan size; since certain expenses incurred in investigating and servicing loans remain relatively fixed regardless of loan size, operating costs as a percentage of loans outstanding should be lower the larger the average loan size. Second, cost ratios were expected to be lower the larger the company, under the presumption that significant economies of size might exist in consumer lending. Third, the cost ratios were expected to rise with increases in net charge-offs to average outstandings because charge-offs reflect the degree of risk inherent in companies' loan portfolios; the higher the risk, the higher the costs associated with loan collection activities. Fourth, it was anticipated that the operating cost ratios would be higher when the proportion of new borrowers to old borrowers is higher because of management's better insights and related judgments in lending to the latter; the costs of investigating loan applications are lower for previous borrowers. Fifth, since certain operating costs are relatively constant, the operating-cost ratios, other things equal, were expected to decline with increases in the number of loans outstanding per loan office. Finally, it was anticipated that the cost ratios differ because of variations in the types of business activities in which the sample companies engage. For example, there are differences among the sample companies regarding the degree of concentration in lending versus nonlending and business activities. Additionally, differences exist among the companies regarding the degree of specialization in small loans versus other types of loans. Therefore, sixth and seventh company characteristics were introduced to account for differences in the cost ratios attributable to differences in the degree and nature of company lending activities.

The analysis here has been purposefully restricted to "operating costs" of the sample companies—that is, to wage and salary expenses, advertising and promotional outlays, recognized losses, and "other operating expenses." Aside from these operating costs, the sample companies make substantial outlays to pay interest on borrowed funds and to meet their federal tax obligations. These debt-servicing and federal outlays are purposely ignored until Chapter V because the factors which influence the size of these outlays are not closely related to the factors which affect the costs of making small loans. The relative size of a company's federal tax liability is primarily a function of the company's tax bracket, and the amount of interest paid for borrowed funds depends largely on the proportion of debt in the company's capital structure. Hence the relative sizes of a company's federal tax and debt-servicing outlays are primarily related to factors different from the factors affecting the operating costs of making small loans. In Chapter V the factors affecting the costs of borrowed funds (debt-servicing costs) are analyzed in detail.

Operating costs tell only part of the story. It is a generally accepted economic axiom that companies should not attempt to minimize costs, but rather should aspire to maximize profits. For this reason the analysis is not limited to costs. After the relations between various company characteristics and operating costs are analyzed, the focus of attention is shifted to revenues. Following the same pattern as for operating costs, the relation between the identified company characteristics and gross income is examined. In a concluding step the operating-cost and revenue relationships are integrated, thereby enabling the reader to perceive the relation between the various company characteristics and operating profits.[9]

The Evidence

Statistical experimentation has suggested that among the seven company characteristics alluded to earlier in the chapter, three characteristics best account for variations in both operating costs and gross income among the forty-eight sample companies.[10] These are (1) average loan size (X_1), (2) a surrogate for loan risk (X_2), and (3) the loan mix, representing sales finance and business loans as a percentage of total loans (X_3).

Operating-Cost Ratios and Average Loan Size

Variations in average loan size (X_1) among the sample companies are more closely associated with differences in the operating-cost ratios

[9] Operating profits are defined as gross income minus operating costs before interest and taxes. The terms "operating profits" and "EBIT" (Earnings Before Interest and Taxes) are used interchangeably.

[10] That is to say, a regression function could be derived using these three independent variables and operating-cost ratios or gross-income ratios which is optimal in the sense that (1) the multiple correlation coefficient, adjusted for degrees of freedom, is maximized; (2) obvious evidence of multicollinearity is avoided; and (3) the list of company characteristics is restricted to those which proved to be statistically significant at the .05 level.

The remaining four characteristics did not appear to be closely related to variations in operating costs or gross income among the companies except in special respects which are discussed later.

(Y_1) than are variations in the other two characteristics. The relationship between all three company characteristics enumerated in the preceding paragraph and the operating-cost ratios can be expressed in the form of a regression equation which indicates the net relation between operating costs and average loan size when the effects on operating costs of loan risk (X_2) and the ratio of sales finance and business loans to total loans (X_3) have been statistically removed. The average association between operating costs per \$100 of loans outstanding and average loan size for the sample companies during 1962–64 is depicted in Chart 8.

Chart 8 shows the variation in cost ratios unexplained by the other two company characteristics $(X_2$ and $X_3)$, which is explained by differing average loan sizes (X_1) among the companies. The points plotted around the average loan size/operating-cost line reveal that not all of the differences in operating costs among the sample companies are explained by average loan size or by X_2 and X_3. If these three variables were capable of explaining *all* the variation in the operating-cost ratios, each of the forty-eight companies' operating cost values would be plotted on the average loan size/operating-cost line. In reality the three analyzed variables account for 60 per cent of the variation in the operating-cost ratios among the sample companies.[11] The association between average loan size and the operating-cost percentages depicted in the chart is statistically significant at the .01 level—that is, there is less than one chance in a hundred that the observed results could have been obtained as a consequence of random sampling errors.

The line in Chart 8 indicates that operating costs as a percentage of loans outstanding decline by \$1.26 on the average with each \$100 increase in average loan size, after eliminating the effects of X_2 and X_3 on costs. The observed effect of average loan size on operating cost

---

[11] Given the available data, it obviously was not possible to include all company characteristics presumed to influence the cost percentages. Certain company characteristics were excluded from the analysis even though they were hypothesized to be influential determinants. For example, the ratio of the number of loan applications processed by a company to the number of loans actually made undoubtedly influences the specific cost percentage; the processing of loan applications is costly, and hence the higher the proportion of loan applications to loans actually made, the higher the operating costs as a per cent of loans outstanding. This variable could not be included due to data limitations. Because certain characteristics have remained unidentified or have been excluded due to data limitations, it is **not** surprising that a substantial proportion of variation in the cost ratios remains unexplained.

CHART 8

Average Loan Size and Operating-Cost Ratios, 1962–64

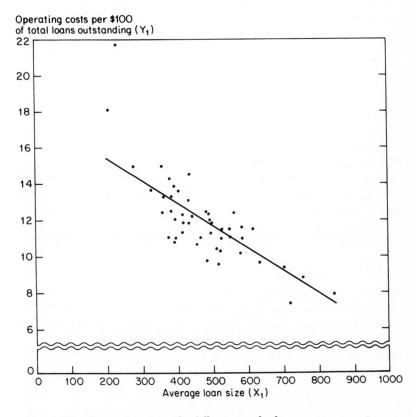

Operating costs per $100
of total loans outstanding (Y₁)

Average loan size (X₁)

NOTE: This chart is based on the following multiple regression equation:

$$Y_1 = .1779 - 1.262\,X_1 + 1.4808\,X_2 - .0519\,X_3,$$

where Y_1 is operating costs per $100 of loans outstanding, X_1 is average loan size in hundreds of dollars, X_2 is net charge-offs as a percentage of average outstandings, and X_3 is business and sales finance loans as a percentage of total loans. The multiple correlation coefficient for this equation is .79 and the r^2 adjusted for degrees of freedom is .60. Variables X_1 and X_2 are significant at the .01 level and X_3 is significant at the .05 level.

The line is derived from the partial regression equation which portrays the relation between Y_1 and X_1. This equation is obtained by holding X_2 and X_3 constant at their mean values.

The dots are the residuals for each observation, not the actual observations themselves.

percentages is not surprising. Several types of operating costs—expenses incurred in investigating and servicing loans—do not change appreciably with changes in the average size of a loan which a company makes. The larger a company's average loan size, the fewer loans it must process to achieve a given level of outstandings. Therefore, companies whose average loan sizes are high incur comparatively low operating costs as a percentage of loans outstanding, other things equal.[12]

Operating-Cost Ratios and Loan Risk

As indicated earlier, variations in the operating cost ratios are more closely associated with variations in average loan size (X_1) than with variations in either the loan risk (X_2) or loan mix (X_3) variables.[13] The loan risk variable, however, is also quite important. This company characteristic, which is in reality the ratio of net charge-offs to average outstandings, is a proxy for loan risk. Chart 9 depicts the average relation between operating costs per $100 of loans outstanding (Y_1) and loan risk (X_2).

The upward slope of the line indicates that the ratio of operating costs to loans outstanding is higher for companies with higher charge-off ratios, after the effects on costs of average loan size and the ratio of business and sales finance loans to total loans have been removed. On the average, operating costs per hundred for the sample companies increase $1.48 with each per cent increase in loan risk. The loan risk variable is itself one component of operating costs.[14] Moreover, ad-

[12] The reader is cautioned that this conclusion does not mean that operating profits are necessarily lower for companies characterized by low average loan size. The ultimate effect on profitability of average loan size cannot be gauged until after the relation between average loan size and gross income per $100 of loans outstanding has also been explored; company profits depend not only on costs but also on income. The effect of average loan size on gross income and ultimately on company profitability is examined in a subsequent section.

[13] The simple correlation coefficient between operating costs as a percentage of loans outstanding and average loan size is $-.65$.

[14] There is an identification problem resulting from the inclusion of X_2 in the estimating equation since the dependent variable (Y_1) also includes "losses" as one of its elements. For two reasons this problem is not considered serious. First, a test of the association between X_2 and Y_1, after removing "losses" from Y_1, has revealed that Y_1 and X_2 remain highly correlated. Second, "losses" represent less than 15 per cent of operating costs for the average sample company: X_2 is only similar in definition to a small fraction of the elements comprising Y_1.

CHART 9

Net Charge-Offs as Percentage of Average Loans Outstanding and Operating Cost Ratios, 1962–64

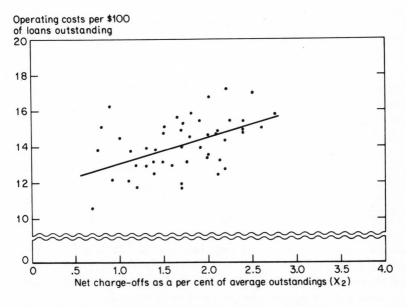

NOTE: Based on the following multiple regression equation:

$$Y_1 = .1779 - 1.262 \, X_1 + 1.4808 \, X_2 - .0519 \, X_3.$$

See Chart 8 for other details.

ditional resources are required to service and to collect delinquent loans as loan risk increases. It is, therefore, understandable that higher operating costs per $100 of loans outstanding accompany higher degrees of loan risk, other things equal.

Operating-Cost Ratios and Loan Mix

Obviously, the costs incurred by small-loan companies apply not only to small loans—that is, to the cash loans in which this study is primarily interested— but also to the nonlending and to the sales finance and business lending activities of each company. Small loans constitute 78 per cent of total assets for the average sample company during the 1962–64 period. Because reported costs pertain to all company activities, it has been necessary to separate the effects of costs applicable to small-loan activities from costs pertaining to other facets of company operations.

It was ascertained by statistical experimentation that cost percentages during 1962–64 for the sample companies were not significantly related to the loan-to-asset ratio (X_5). In other words, cost ratios were not systematically higher or lower for the sample companies during 1962–64 according to the proportion of total loans to total assets. On the other hand, tests suggested that the proportion of sales finance credit and business loans to total loans (X_3) is significantly related to costs; and therefore, in order to analyze costs pertaining to small-loan activities, it has been necessary to include X_3 in the multiple regression analysis in order to remove statistically the influence of this variable on costs. This variable accounts for 9 per cent of the explained variation in the operating cost ratios which is unexplained either by average loan size (X_1) or by loan risk (X_2).

Chart 10 shows the relation between the operating cost ratios and X_3 after the influence of average loan size and loan risk on the cost ratios has been removed. As revealed by the downward slope of the line, increases in the proportion of sales finance and business loans in the loan mix are accompanied by declines in operating costs. An average decline of $.05 in the cost ratios is associated with each percentage increase in sales finance and business loans. It typically costs less per dollar of credit to investigate sales finance and business loan applications than their small-loan counterparts. Additionally, collection expenses per dollar of outstandings for these types of loans as well as loss rates tend to be lower than for small loans. In view of these considerations, it is not surprising that companies with relatively large proportions of sales finance and business loans in their portfolios incur lower operating costs in relation to loans outstanding.

Gross Income and Operating-Profit Relationships

Gross income for the sample companies consists of finance charges on receivables, income from insurance sold to customers, and earnings from other company activities. Gross income ratios for each company (Y_2) are obtained by expressing gross income for the 1962–64 period

CHART 10

Business and Sales Finance Loans as Percentage of Total Loans Outstanding and Operating Cost Ratios, 1962–64

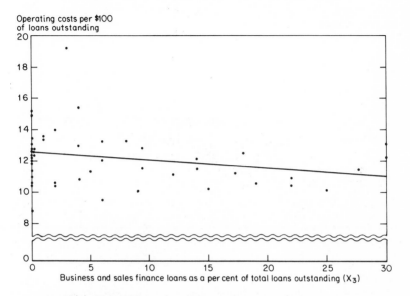

NOTE: Based on the following multiple regression equation:

$$Y_1 = .1779 - 1.262\ X_1 + 1.4808\ X_2 - .0519\ X_3.$$

See Chart 8 for other details.

as a percentage of year-end outstandings for the period. Variations in these gross income ratios among the sample companies are best explained by an estimating equation which includes the same company characteristics included earlier in the operating cost equation.[15]

Gross Income Ratios and Average Loan Size

Chart 11 depicts the average relation between the gross income ratio and average loan size, after the effects of loan risk and loan mix

[15] Although all seven identified company characteristics were free to enter the gross income estimating equation, only the regression coefficients of average loan size, loan risk, and the ratio of business and sales finance loans to total loans— the same independent variables included in the operating cost equation—were significant at the .05 level.

CHART 11

Average Loan Size and Gross Income per $100 of Loans Outstanding, 1962–64

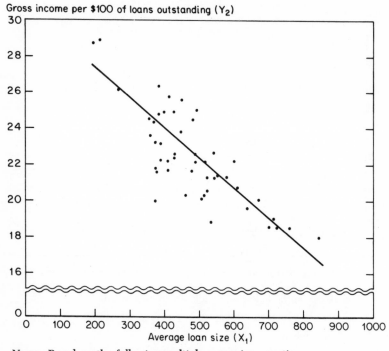

NOTE: Based on the following multiple regression equation:

$$Y_2 = .2941 - 1.706\ X_1 + 1.1034\ X_2 - .0695\ X_3,$$

where Y_2 is gross income per $100 of loans outstanding and the other variables are defined as in Chart 8. The multiple correlation coefficient for this equation is .75 and the r^2, adjusted for degrees of freedom, is .53. The regression coefficient for X_1 is significant at the .01 level and the regression coefficients for X_2 and X_3 are significant at the .05 level. The line is derived from the partial regression equation which portrays the relation between Y_2 and X_1. This equation is obtained by holding X_2 and X_3 constant at their mean values. The plotted points are the residuals of the observations, not the actual observations themselves.

on gross income have been eliminated. The line of gross income to average loan size slopes downward to the right, with gross income per $100 of loans outstanding declining, on the average, $1.71 with each $100 increase in average loan size. The small-loan laws in most states impose different loan ceilings and permit consumer finance companies to charge higher rates on smaller loans. Hence, because of differences in loan size, ceilings, and rates among the states, it is logical that the gross income ratios are inversely associated with average loan size.

Operating-Profit Ratios and Average Loan Size

The respective lines for gross income to average loan size and operating costs to average loan size are combined in the top panel of Chart 12. Inspection of this panel reveals a high degree of apparent correlation between the gross income ratios and the operating cost ratios. When gross income per $100 of loans outstanding is high, operating costs per $100 of loans are high, and vice versa.[16] High gross income ratios are achieved by companies characterized by low average loan sizes, and these companies incur higher operating costs per dollar of outstandings, for reasons noted earlier. There is another plausible explanation for the close association between the gross income ratios and the operating cost ratios. It may be that the higher gross income ratios themselves permit certain small-loan companies to incur higher operating costs. For example, a company with comparatively high gross income in relation to loans outstanding may at its own discretion spend more on advertising or be more willing to accept added risk.

As revealed in the top panel of Chart 12 both operating costs and gross income decline sharply as average loan size increases. The lower operating costs which accompany large average loan sizes, however are more than offset by associated declines in gross income. This phenomenon is revealed by the gradual tendency in the top panel for the operating cost and gross income lines to converge as loan size increases; it suggests that larger loans are somewhat less profitable than smaller loans, as indicated by the moderate downward slope of the EBIT line in the bottom panel.

The bottom panel of the chart depicts the net relation between operating profits per $100 of loans outstanding (EBIT) and average loan size for the sample companies. The EBIT variable (Y_3) is obtained for each company by subtracting 1962–64 operating costs (Y_1) from 1962–64 gross income (Y_2). The line in the bottom panel depicts the average relation between the EBIT ratios and average loan size, holding constant the number of loans per office (X_4), the proportion of

---

[16] The simple r between the gross income ratios and the operating costs ratios is .91.

CHART 12

Average Loan Size and Operating Costs, Gross Income, and EBIT per $100 of Loans Outstanding, 1962–64

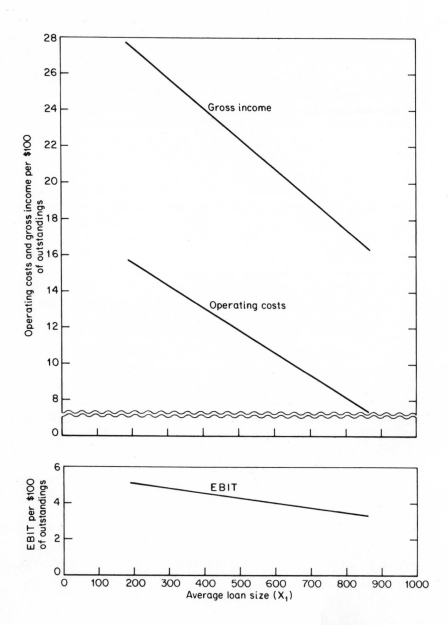

NOTE TO CHART 12

The multiple regression equations on which the lines in the top panel are based are explained in the notes to Chart 11 and 8, respectively. The bottom panel is based on the following multiple regression equation:

$$Y_3 = .1444 - 0.289\,X_1 - .1051\,X_2 - .0105\,X_3 + 1.089\,X_4 - .0884\,X_5 + .0057\,X_6,$$

where Y_3 equals the ratio of EBIT to loans outstanding, X_6 is the log of total assets to the base 10, X_4 and X_5 are as defined previously. The multiple correlation coefficient is .71 and the r^2 adjusted for degrees of freedom is .43. The regression coefficient for X_1 on which the line in the bottom panel is based is -0.289 and its standard error is 0.176. This equation is obtained when the standard of excluding variables not significant at the .05 level is relaxed. (Variables X_1, X_2, and X_3 are excluded from regressions on Y_3 when the list of dependent variables is restricted to those which prove to be statistically significant at the .05 level.) Although the gradual convergence of the operating cost and gross income lines in the top panel visually supports the implication of the bottom panel that gradual declines in EBIT ratios accompany increases in average loan size, the slope of the EBIT line in the bottom panel could have resulted due to chance.

total loans to total assets (X_5), and average loan size (X_1) loan risk (X_2) and loan mix (X_3).[17]

The implication of the EBIT line is that larger average loan sizes are accompanied by somewhat lower operating profit ratios, other things equal. It is interesting to note in this connection that average loan size for the sample companies increased from $411 in 1962 to $454 in 1963 to $493 in 1964. Although the coefficient on which the moderately downward-sloping EBIT line is based is not significant at the .05 level, the suggested implication that increases in average loan size exert downward pressure on EBIT is consistent with the nine-company trend through time noted in Chapter II.

Have the sample companies characterized by relatively large average loan sizes experienced a squeeze in profit margins? This question cannot be answered unequivocally. Yet both the slope and goodness of fit of the EBIT line leave room for doubt. Although a company's operating costs and gross income are both dramatically influenced by average loan size, the most important variable—operating profits per $100 of loans—is relatively insensitive to changes in average loan size as revealed by the comparatively gradual downward slope of the EBIT line in Chart 13. Moreover, the mild downward slope of the

[17] The two additional variables, X_4 nor X_5, are included in the EBIT estimating equation because of their statistically significant relation with the EBIT ratios (Y_3). These variables were excluded from both the operating cost and gross income estimating equations because in the analysis of variations in Y_1 and Y_2 neither X_4 nor X_5 was found to be closely related to the dependent variables.

average loan size/EBIT line could have occurred due to chance.[18] Thus, the degree of company concentration in small versus large loans does not appear to be an important determinant of operating profitability.

Moreover, it may be that *other things do not remain equal* among companies with larger average loan sizes, although evidence on this point is inconclusive. Specifically, higher average loan sizes may be accompanied by lower loan risk.[19] And slightly higher EBIT ratios are associated with lower levels of loan risk, as the next section indicates. Hence the tendency for larger average loan sizes to accompany lower EBIT ratios may be offset at least in part by lower levels of loan risk.

It is important that the above-mentioned implications regarding the relation of the EBIT ratios and average loan size be interpreted broadly. The conclusions apply to average operating conditions for all states in which the sample companies operate, since the basic data aggregate each company's operating costs and revenues among the states in which the company has offices. In reality, the small-loan companies are confronted with different gross income and operating cost ratios in each state by virtue of differences which exist in legally permissible rate structures and loan size ceilings.

Operating-Profit Ratios and Loan Risk

Chart 13 depicts the relation between the loan risk variable (X_2) and the gross income ratios for the sample companies during the 1962–64 period, after the effects on revenues of average loan size and the ratio of sales finance and business loans to total loans have been removed. The line suggests that the gross income ratios on the average are $1.10 higher per hundred when net charge-offs as a percentage of average outstandings are higher by $1 per hundred.

In view of the fact that small-loan companies usually charge the maximum rates permitted in each state, a question arises concerning why higher gross income rates are associated with higher levels of

[18] The average loan size variable is not sufficiently powerful to enter the EBIT estimating equation when the equation is restricted to variables significant at the .05 level.

[19] The simple r between average loan size and loan risk is $-.23$. Thus there is some evidence of an inverse association between X_1 and X_2, although the coefficient is not significant at the .05 level.

CHART 13

Portfolio Risk and Gross Income, 1962–64

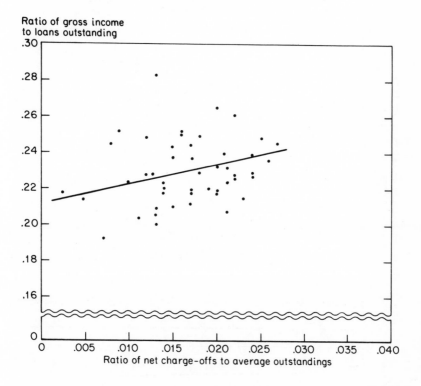

Ratio of gross income to loans outstanding

Ratio of net charge-offs to average outstandings

NOTE: Based on the same estimating equation as Chart 11. The line is derived from the partial regression equation which portrays the relation between X_2 and Y_2. This equation is obtained by holding variables X_1 and X_3 constant at their mean values. The plotted points are residuals, not actual values.

loan risk (when average loan size is held constant). This observation can probably be traced to the activities of companies whose lending activities are concentrated in specific states. In states where comparatively high rates of charge and low loan ceilings are permitted, companies will accept, on balance, riskier loan portfolios. One might therefore expect both gross income and net charge-off ratios to be

CHART 14

Net Charge-Offs as Percentage of Average Outstandings and Operating Costs, Gross Income, and EBIT per $100 of Loans Outstanding, 1962–64

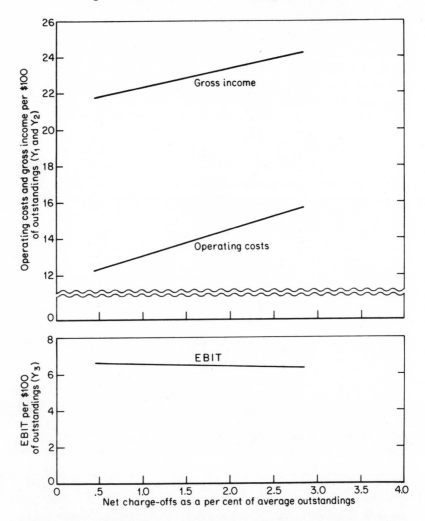

NOTE: The multiple regression equations on which the lines in the top panel are based are explained in the notes to Charts 13 and 9 respectively. The bottom panel is based on the EBIT estimating equation used for Chart 12. The regression coefficient for X_2 on which the line in the bottom panel is based is −.1051 and its standard error is .2155.

higher for companies concentrating in such states. Similarly, in states characterized by comparatively low rate structures and large loan ceilings, lenders accept lower average risks in the extension of credit; companies concentrating in these states might well experience lower charge-off ratios as well as lower gross income ratios.

In the bottom panel of Chart 14 the relation between loan risk and the EBIT ratios is depicted after the influence of the other independent variables on the EBIT ratios has been removed. The EBIT line slopes moderately downward to the right, revealing that higher degrees of loan risk are accompanied by slightly lower EBIT ratios. Again, the relation between variations in loan risk and EBIT is not strong enough to rule out the possibility of the down-sloping EBIT line in the bottom panel resulting due to chance.[20]

CHART 15

Business and Sales Finance Loans as Percentage of Total Loans and Gross Income per $100 of Outstandings, 1962–64

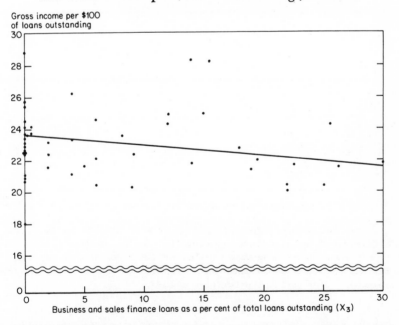

NOTE: See the note to Chart 11 for the multiple regression equation on which this chart is based.

[20] The risk variable is not sufficiently powerful to enter the EBIT estimating equation when the equation is restricted to variables significant at the .05 level.

CHART 16

Business Loans and Sales Finance Credit as Percentage of Total Loans and Operating Costs, Gross Income, and EBIT per $100 of Outstandings, 1962–64

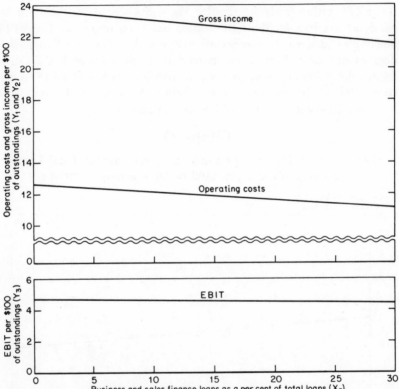

NOTE: The multiple regression equations on which the lines in the top panel are based are explained in the notes to Charts 10 and 15 respectively. The bottom panel is based on the estimating equation for EBIT described in the notes to Chart 12. The regression coefficient for X_3 on which the line in the bottom panel is based is −.0105 and its standard error is .0141.

By far the most important feature of Chart 14 concerns the extent to which higher costs accompanying higher degrees of loan risk are offset by higher gross income percentages. The gross income and operating cost lines in the top panel are almost parallel. Although an important determinant of both operating costs and gross income, loan risk (like average loan size) provides only nominal insights into variations in the EBIT percentages among the companies.

Operating-Profit Ratios and Loan Mix

As noted in the preceding section, the ratio of business and sales finance loans to total loans is an important determinant of variations in operating costs among the sample companies. This variable is also important in explaining variations in the gross income ratios among the companies. Chart 15 depicts the relation between business and sales finance loans as a percentage of total loans (X_3) and the gross income ratios during the 1962–64 period after the influence on gross income of average loan size and loan risk has been removed. The line, which slopes downward to the right, indicates that the gross income ratios, on the average, decline $.07 with each percentage increase in the proportion of business and sales finance loans. This result is not surprising since the sales finance and business loans typically bear lower rates than small loans. As the proportion of the loan mix in the form of business and sales finance loans increases, income per $100 of outstandings declines.

The top panel of Chart 16 portrays differences in loan mix in relation to gross income and operating cost ratios. Again, the most significant characteristic of the graph concerns the extent to which the declines in operating costs associated with higher proportions of sales finance and business loans are paralleled by declines in gross income. The result is an EBIT line in the bottom panel which is almost horizontal, suggesting that the EBIT ratios among the companies are fairly insensitive to the proportion of business and sales finance loans in the loan mix.[21] The EBIT line has a very gradual downward slope that shows the .01 per cent average decline in the EBIT percentages which accompanies each percentage increase in the proportion of business and sales finance loans.

By way of summary, it is important to note that the income and cost differences associated with variations in average loan size, loan risks, and loan mix are largely offsetting among the forty-eight companies. Consequently, the EBIT ratios are not very sensitive to varia-

[21] As in the case of the risk and average loan size variables, X_3 is not sufficiently powerful to enter the EBIT estimating equation when the equation is restricted to variables significant at the .05 level.

tions in these company characteristics. It is necessary to look elsewhere for factors associated with major differences in operating
profitability.

Operating-Profit Ratios and Number of Loans per Office

The most important identified characteristic associated with differences among the companies in the EBIT ratios is the number of
loans outstanding per loan office (X_4). Although the relation between
X_4 and Y_1 was not sufficiently strong for X_4 to be included in the
operating cost estimating equation, variations in X_4 are closely associated with the salary component of operating costs. There is also
an apparent tendency for the gross income ratios to be higher with
larger number of loans per office.[22] If the composition of loans outstanding remained unchanged as the number of loans per office increased, rates of charge (the gross income ratios) would remain
constant. Yet there is a significant inclination for companies with relatively high levels of loan office activity to have loans of comparatively
small average size.[23] Several factors may help to explain this inverse
relation between average loan size and the number of loans outstanding per office. First, it may be that offices attract a larger proportion of
smaller borrowers as activity levels expand and more attention is de-
voted to the marginal borrower. Second, the tendency may also be
explained in part by differences in loan office average maturities. A
new office is likely to be characterized by a comparatively high average loan size and long average maturity because most of its loans are
new. As repayments occur and the number of accounts expand, the
average loan size automatically declines. Third, the inverse association might be attributed in part to the legal frameworks in densely
populated states, such as New York and New Jersey which have a
high proportion of large national company offices. The combination of
restraints on entry, relatively low rates for small loan sizes, and the
high population densities in such states may require economies of
scale which limit the market to companies who achieve large numbers
of loans per office. Regardless of its precise origin, gross income per

---

[22] Of necessity, conclusions regarding the slope of the gross income/number
of loans per office line remain tentative. X_4 was not powerful enough to enter the
gross income estimating equation.

[23] Support for this assertion can be found in the $-.35$ simple r between average loan size and number of loans outstanding per office. The coefficient is
significant at the .05 level.

CHART 17

Number of Loans Outstanding per Office and EBIT per $100 of Loans Outstanding, 1962–64

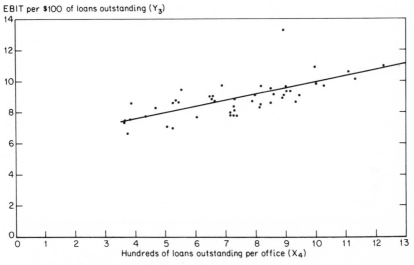

EBIT per $100 of loans outstanding (Y_3)

Hundreds of loans outstanding per office (X_4)

NOTE: based on the following estimating equation:

$$Y_3 = .1293 + .0393 \, X_4 - .0844 \, X_5,$$

where each of the variables is defined as previously. The multiple correlation coefficient is .64 and the r^2, adjusted for degrees of freedom, is .38. The regression coefficients for X_4 and X_5 are significant at the .01 level. The line is obtained from the partial regression coefficient which portrays the relation between Y_3 and X_4. To obtain this equation, X_5 is held constant at its mean value. The dots are the residuals of the observations, not the actual observations themselves.

$100 of outstandings tends to be higher for companies characterized by high levels of loan activity.

Thus the operating cost ratios are lower and the gross income ratios higher as loans outstanding per office increase. The expense and gross income lines diverge as activity levels expand resulting in the pronounced upward slope of the EBIT line in Chart 17. The line suggests that, on the average, the EBIT ratios increase $.40 with each 100-unit increase in the number of loans outstanding per loan office. The relation is strong, as indicated by the closeness in fit of the plotted residuals.[24]

[24] The regression coefficient for X_4 on which the line in Chart 17 is based is significant at the .01 level. The estimating equation also suggests that the ratio of total loans to total assets (X_5) is an important determinant of EBIT per $100 of loans outstanding. Although X_5 enters the estimating equation, this variable

CHART 18

Simple Correlation Between Number of Loans Outstanding per Office and Company Size

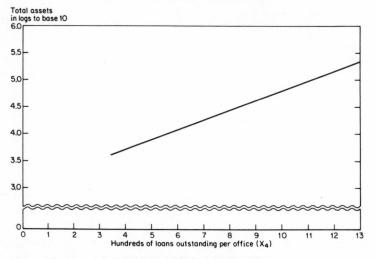

NOTE: The line is based on the following equation:

$$Y_7 = 2.9476 + .0018 \, X_4,$$

where Y_7 is company size in terms of the log of total assets to the base 10 and X_4 is the number of loans per office during 1964. The simple r for the equation is .54 and the r^2 adjusted for degrees of freedom is .27. X_4 is significant at the .01 level.

The simple r's have also been computed for 1963 and 1962. In these instances the regression coefficients for X_4 are .0018 and .0019 respectively. As for the 1964 equation, the regression coefficients for X_4 are significant at the .01 level.

Number of Loans per Office and Company Size

In view of the apparent association between number of loans per office and operating profitability, it is especially significant that large

---

cannot be assigned economic significance because of the manner in which the EBIT ratio is defined. Companies with smaller proportions of loans to total assets naturally have higher total profits (EBIT) in relation to loans. Profits derive from all the assets which a company employs, and a company can automatically be expected to have a high EBIT/loan ratio if loans comprise a comparatively small proportion of total assets. (The reader will recall that X_5 has been allowed to enter the various estimating equations in order to hold the proportion of lending to nonlending activities constant so that the effects of other variables on expenses and revenues could be more clearly perceived.)

companies tend to make more loans per office than small companies. The positive relation between size of company and loans per office is shown in Chart 18. The tendency for large companies to achieve higher outstandings per office is apparent notwithstanding the relatively quick pace of new-office openings of the larger companies during recent years. (The number of loans outstanding in new offices is typically low, and therefore one might expect companies' activity levels to decline during periods of loan-office expansion, other things equal.)[25]

There are several plausible explanations for the larger companies' advantage in level of activity. These companies may be in a better position to secure loan-office locations where levels of activity are likely to be high. Some of the larger companies retain experts on demographic conditions who may be better able to select choice locations. With or without experts, the larger companies have an advantage in spotting potentially desirable loan-office locations, given their broader regional or national perspectives. Having decided which loan-office locations are likely to yield high levels of activity, the larger companies are better able to secure leases for these locations by virtue of their established reputations and comparatively strong financial positions. Unquestionably, the advertising media and coverage of the larger companies assist in the achievement of comparatively high activity levels. Finally, the larger companies may be better able to hire, train, and motivate loan-office managers to generate comparatively high levels of volume.

Due to the strong positive association between company size and number of loans per office, large companies realize comparatively high operating profits. The simple r between company size and the EBIT ratios is .47. This significant positive association between company size and the EBIT ratios exists despite the fact that neither the operating cost ratios nor the gross income ratios are significantly influenced by the size variable.

The Assumption of Linearity

Each of the charts has suggested that the dependent variables either decline or increase continuously with variations in the independent variables. There still exists the logical possibility that the dependent

---

[25] The loan-office expansion of the larger companies can be traced to the acquisition of mature offices of other companies as well as to the opening of new offices. One would expect the number of loans per office to be lower only for the new-office component of the expansion.

variables might eventually reach a minimum (or maximum) or begin to increase (or decrease) with further variations in the respective independent variables. This type of possibility is obscured in the charts because the statistical procedures employed assume a linear relation between the various company characteristics and the dependent variables. The question whether or not this assumption is reasonable, given the data for the sample companies, remains to be answered.

The key to this question is found in the dots which are plotted around the net regression lines in each of the charts. As noted earlier, these dots represent variations in each company's operating costs, gross income, or operating profits which are not explained by the variables included in the analysis. If the respective dependent variables reached turning points or stopped declining (or rising), the dots would tend to form U-shaped patterns around the regression lines based on the estimating equations. There are no strong indications of curvilinear relationships, although some are logically plausible. Over the ranges where there are numerous observations for each variable, the dots are rather evenly distributed on both sides of the regression lines. There appear to be no critical turning points within the ranges for which numerous observations are available. Hence the straight-line equations on which the charts are based seem to be fairly good empirical statements of the relation between the independent and the dependent variables.[26]

Summary and Implications of the Findings

Through statistical testing it has been found that, among identified small loan company characteristics, average loan size, loan risk, and business and sales finance loans as a percentage of loan mix are most closely associated with variations in operating costs and gross income. Other things equal, operating costs per $100 of loans outstanding are low when average loan size or the ratio of business and sales finance loans to total loans is large. Also, low operating cost ratios accompany comparatively low degrees of loan risk.

Yet the differences in operating costs accompanying variations **in**

[26] Statistical attempts were made to improve upon the straight-line equations by fitting curvilinear functions to the variables. These experiments were generally unsuccessful in the sense that the multiple correlation coefficients for the estimating equations could not be materially improved by use of the various curvilinear functions.

these factors are largely canceled by offsetting variations in gross income. Like operating costs, gross income per hundred of outstandings is typically low when average loan size is large or when the proportion of sales finance and business loans in the loan mix is high; and high degrees of loan risk are associated with high gross income ratios.

Due to the compensating effects of operating costs and gross income in relation to loans outstanding, differences among the sample companies in net operating income (EBIT) do not appear to accompany differences in average loan sizes, types, or risk characteristics. The *empirical* findings regarding the revenue and cost effects of average loan size, loan risk, and loan mix imply that existing rate structures permit fairly similar rates of operating profit regardless of companies' average loan size, net charge-off experience, or loan composition. It should be re-emphasized, however, that this analysis has focused on companies many of which operate loan offices in numerous states. In reality these multistate firms are confronted with different rate structures, not a single composite rate structure. Important differences in rate structures among the states which in fact provide inducements for making loans of particular types may remain undetected. For this reason it is necessary to examine activities in each state separately to obtain significant insights into the effects of different rate structures on lending activities. In the next chapter, lending behavior is analyzed under small-loan legislation in individual states.

Evidence presented in Chapter II has suggested that during the past fifteen years consumer finance companies have experienced two types of pressures. On the one hand, operating costs per $100 of loans outstanding have decreased. On the other, gross income in relation to loans outstanding has declined more. These trends have had an adverse effect on operating profitability. A most important question with which Chapter II has dealt concerns whether these trends are likely to continue. An equally important, related question concerns whether profits can be maintained even if the rate of decline in gross income ratios continues to exceed the rate of decline in operating cost ratios. The findings contained in this chapter regarding structural characteristics of the companies provide clues to this latter question.

The number of loans outstanding per office for the average sample company dropped from 752 in 1962 to 748 in 1963 and to 736 in 1964. The declining levels of activity can be attributed in large part to the numerous new office openings which occurred during this period. In effect, the rate of new openings exceeded the rate of increased loan demand and, as a consequence, a moderate decline in lending activity per office resulted. This trend is particularly significant in view of this chapter's finding that operating profits are positively associated with the number of loans per office. Higher operating profits are realized by those small-loan companies capable of extending relatively large numbers of loans per office.

An equally important conclusion of this chapter concerns the apparent advantage of large companies in achieving high degrees of loan office utilization. Although differences in company size are not closely associated with variations in the operating cost or gross income ratios, the size variable is significantly correlated with the number of loans per office, which in turn has an important influence on the EBIT ratios. As a consequence, there is a significant positive association between company size and the EBIT ratios.

IV

State Regulation and the Provision of Small Loans

ROBERT P. SHAY

Graduate School of Business,
Columbia University

Introduction

The wide variety of regulatory provisions in laws governing small loans among the states enables a comparison of the way in which differences in state legislation are associated with differences in operating earnings, costs and loan services supplied to borrowers. There is considerable uniformity in the protective philosophy underlying most small-loan statutes, resulting from the influence of the Uniform Small-Loan Law. Yet the scope and coverage of state small-loan laws differ widely. The variety of regulatory provisions necessarily results in differences in risks assumed, the profitability of operations, and the number of borrowers served under the protective features of these laws. The objective of this chapter is to identify aspects of regulation which condition the market for small loans and affect the quantity of loan services provided borrowers.

Summary of Findings

The evidence of this chapter indicates that ceilings on rates and size of loan, the presence of ancillary laws, and the power to restrain entry appear to affect the market for small loans in the thirty states investigated. First, it was observed that when laws restrict loan size and permit relatively high rates of charge, the average risk assumed by the lender tends to be higher, but operating profits, measured by net operating income per $100 of average loans outstanding, are not correspondingly higher. The reason that operating profits are not systematically different appears to be due to the tendency for lenders to adjust operating expenses incurred, including the provision for losses, to the desired rate of gross income allowable under the statute. Second, operating expenses per $100 of average loans outstanding tend to be lower in states where the number of loans per office is larger. This raises the questions: What factors are responsible for increasing the number of loans per office? Is a large demand for small-loan service being met, as indicated by the low population per loan ratio? Or is it the relative scarcity of offices, indicated by high population per office ratios? More loans per office in a state typically occur in states where the population per office is high. But since high population per office tends to accompany high population per loan, the proportionate share of the population receiving loans is relatively low in such states. Restraint upon entry through "convenience and advantage" clauses[1] contributes both to the higher population per office ratios and the higher population per loan ratios.[2]

Third, the presence of other loan laws appears to have limited the loan services provided to borrowers under small-loan statutes more in some states than in others. It is likely that the unwillingness of some state legislatures to raise small-loan ceilings has resulted in parallel opportunities for small-loan licensees to lend under other loan laws.[3] Often other loan laws offer consumer finance companies more attractive rates of charge relative to expenses for larger loans and capital is

[1] Convenience and advantage clauses in the state small-loan law give state supervisory authorities discretionary power to reject applications for licensees to establish loan offices on the grounds that the convenience and advantage of the community would not be served by additional offices.

[2] Higher population per loan ratios represent a smaller number of loans per person in a state. Population per loan ratios ranked from low to high will be used to demonstrate a decreasing quantity of loan services supplied under the small-loan laws of thirty states. An alternative measure, per capita loans outstanding, reflects the amount of funds per person outstanding under the small-loan laws. The latter measure is not affected by "doubling up," which occurs when a single borrower obtains more than one small loan.

[3] Other loan laws were designed to provide exemptions from the usury laws for institutions other than consumer finance companies. They do not extend the same regulatory protection to the borrower as the small-loan statutes.

diverted from smaller loans. Yet several states with other loan laws demonstrate that the presence of an ancillary law need not result in relatively few loan services being offered under the small-loan statute.

Fourth, the six states with the highest population per office ratios and tight restraint upon new offices all ranked relatively low in small-loan services rendered, suggesting that the administration of convenience and advantage clauses may have contributed to a lessening of small-loan services in these states. Thus, although tight restraint on entry may contribute to lower expenses, it would appear that it also adversely affects the availability of small-loan services.

Finally, supplementary insights were gained into the operations of the four largest consumer finance companies under the small-loan laws. It was noted that these companies tend to have larger average size of loans outstanding, lower gross income and operating expense ratios, and higher net operating income ratios per $100 of average loans outstanding than other licensed lenders in the thirty states. That these companies provide mobility to the flow of capital among the states was indicated by their tendency to allocate a larger proportion of their funds to states where operating profits were higher and where the number of loans per office was larger. As a result they were able to obtain a larger share of the market.

The Basic Data and Concepts

Information was gathered from the 1964 state reports for all licensees operating under small-loan statutes in thirty states.[4] Consumer finance company operations under larger loan laws in thirteen states are not included in the basic data because most such information is not readily comparable and not always available.[5]

Income and expense data are expressed either as "dollars per $100 of average loans outstanding" or as "dollars per loan account," as indicated below:

Gross income—gross operating income, typically including finance charges, income from insurance, other charges, and recoveries from loans previously charged off.

[4] Consumer finance companies have to obtain a license for each branch office in most states.

[5] Other loan statutes were not modeled on the uniform small-loan law, and reporting practices vary. Reporting practices under the state small-loan laws generally follow the model law, which makes available considerable information in a common form.

Operating expenses—total operating expenses less any interest charges and income taxes.

Net operating income—gross operating income less operating expenses as defined above.

Other concepts utilized in the analysis of this chapter include:

Average loans outstanding—the simple average of beginning- and end-of-year loans outstanding.

Average number of loans—simple average of the number of beginning- and end-of-year loans outstanding.

Average size of loan—the average amount of loans outstanding divided by the average number of loans.

Risks assumed—the ratio of bad debts per $100 of average loans outstanding. In the state reports, bad debts are reported either as provision for losses or losses charged off. Reporting practices vary from company to company.

Average number of loans per office—the number of offices in a state divided into the average number of loans outstanding. The reporting dates when offices are counted vary among the states, but typically are in the latter part of the year.

Population per office—the number of offices in a state divided into the 1964 population of the state. This measure reflects differences in the administration of convenience and advantage clauses in addition to other factors, including population density.

Population per loan—the average number of loans divided into the 1964 population of the state. This was used as the primary measure of loan service supplied in any state and was ranked from low to high to reflect the larger to smaller quantities of loan services among the states.

Per capita loans outstanding—the average loans outstanding divided by the 1964 population of the state. This was presented as an alternative measure of loan service since it reflects the average amount of loans, rather than the number, in relation to the population.

Per capita income—personal income in a state divided by the population of the state.

Urban ratio—1960 ratio of the number of persons in communities of 2,500 or more to the total state population.

Most of the tables are based upon state reports. In addition, facsimiles of data reported to the state authorities and supplementary information were obtained from the four largest consumer finance companies (Household Finance Corporation, Beneficial Management Corporation, Seaboard Finance Corporation, and American Investment Company). This information was used for preliminary statistical investigation and to obtain supplementary insights into income and expense relations among the states.[6]

Data reported to state supervisory authorities are far from ideal for shedding light upon the subject of our research. As a proxy for the average level of rate of charge in a state, it was necessary to use gross operating income, which includes income from insurance, other charges, and recoveries as well. Often these items are not broken down separately, and there is no certainty that the same items are included in residual categories. In some states insurance income is included with other business categories, some states subtract it from expenses and delete it from income, and others do not say what procedures are followed.

The decision not to study total operating expense components (other than the bad-debt ratio) was made because of the diversity of accounting practices followed in making allocations of expense components. While it remains true that total operating expenses are also affected by the manner in which companies operating in more than one state allocate expenses *among* states, the proportionate effect upon total expenses would not be expected to be as great as upon individual components. In thirteen of the thirty states there is a separate problem of allocating expenses between loans made under the small-loan statute and those made under other (typically larger-loan) statutes. Procedures customarily assign some proportion of operating expenses to the small-loan-law report. The proportions vary, but are usually based upon a formula assigning relative weights to the number and amounts of loans. Data are reported on fiscal rather than on calendar years in four states.[7]

---

[6] In particular, it was desirable to investigate income and expense relationships with average loan size free of the influence of allocated regional and home office expenses. Further, average monthly outstandings provided a better estimate than the average of beginning- and end-of-year outstandings available in the state reports. Finally, the companies supplied information that made possible the separation of federal and state income taxes from other taxes in those states whose reports did not provide a breakdown. The procedure followed was to apply the proportion of state/or federal income taxes to total taxes for the four companies as the basis of estimating income taxes for all companies. The result is to overstate taxes and understate expenses, since the large companies are taxed on a higher proportion of income than small companies, but the adjustment appeared more desirable than to ignore the different reporting procedures in the reports.

[7] In Arizona, New Hampshire, and North Dakota, ratios were computed from the fiscal-year reports ending June 30, 1964. In West Virginia, the fiscal year ending June 30, 1965, was used.

Despite the problems inherent in the data, the use of simple correlation analysis and comparison of averages reveal systematic associations and relationships which are consistent with those found in the more accurate four-company data supplied us. Attention was confined to relatively simple techniques partly because of the uneven quality of the data but also because the data do not lend themselves easily to the multiple regression techniques used in Chapter III. For example, the interrelation between permitted rates of charge and loan size ceilings posed a major problem for statistical analysis of operating income and expense data. That most states have their rate structures graduated downward by loan size intervals means that gross income ratios reflect the joint influence of regulatory rate and loan size ceilings, which cannot be separated.

Operating Income and Cost Ratios in Thirty States

Among the thirty states in 1964, the average (mean) gross income, operating cost, and net income ratios per $100 of average loans outstanding were $25.63, $16.56, and $9.06, respectively, as shown in Table 21.[8] The bad-debt portion of the operating expense ratio was $2.96 and the average size of loan was $396. Yet these averages, by themselves, tell us little about the characteristics of income and expenses among the states. The standard deviations shown in Table 21 reveal the degree of variation around the average for each ratio shown. We use the coefficient of variation, the standard deviation divided by the mean, to compare the relative variation for the ratios shown. Thus, it is apparent that operating expense ratios among the states vary more than the corresponding gross and net income ratios. Also, bad-

[8] These figures may be contrasted with the lower gross income, operating expense, and net operating income ratios per $100 of average outstanding consumer receivables in Chapter II: $21.40, $12.73, and $8.67, respectively. There are three reasons for the lower figures shown in the earlier chapter. First, the denominator of the ratios, consumer receivables, is larger than outstanding loans because it includes holdings of consumer sales finance paper. Second, loans made under ancillary statutes, where average loan size is larger, are included in consumer receivables but not in loans outstanding under small-loan statutes. Third, the nine large companies may have larger average loan sizes and correspondingly lower ratios than the smaller companies, as suggested by the comparison of the four largest companies' ratios with those of all companies in the 1964 state reports. See Table 28, below.

TABLE 21

Reported Average Operating Income and Cost Data, Licensed Consumer
Finance Offices in Thirty States, 1964

	Arith-metic Mean	Standard Deviation	Coeffi-cient of Varia-tion[a]	Range of Ratios	
				High	Low
Gross income per $100 of average loans outstanding	$25.63	4.15	16%	$40.70 (Ala.)	$20.20 (N.Y.)
Operating expense per $100 of average loans outstanding	16.56	4.59	28	32.80 (Ala.)	10.70 (N.Y.)
Net operating income[b] per $100 of average loans outstanding	9.06	1.54	17	12.40 (W.Va.)	4.30 (Wisc.)
Bad debts[c] per $100 of average loans outstanding	2.96	1.00	34	6.00 (Ala.)	1.70 (N.H., N.J.)
Average loan size	396	108	27	588 (Ohio)	131 (Ala.)

Note: Calendar years except for New Hampshire, North Dakota, and West Virginia, which are all fiscal years. Maine's calendar year is 1963.

[a] The coefficient of variation is the quotient when the standard deviation is divided by the arithmetic mean.

[b] Before interest and income taxes.

[c] Represented by either provision for losses or losses charged off on state reports. It is a component of operating expense per $100 of average loans outstanding.

debt ratios represent an important part of the variation in expense ratios. Finally, the 27 per cent coefficient of variation in the average loan size partly reflects the wide differences in loan ceilings among the states.

Differences in rate and loan ceilings, as well as other features of small-loan legislation, contribute to the heterogeneity represented in the ratios among different states. By reviewing the range of high and low ratios drawn from the states, it is possible to identify the extent of differences and hazard some reasons for the state to be located at one or the other extreme. Alabama, for example, appears as the state with the highest gross income ratio, the highest bad-debt ratio, and the lowest average loan size. Alabama is one of three states with a $300 ceiling in the small-loan law and an auxiliary law under which licensees also operate. Their maximum rates (per cent per month unless otherwise stated) and loan sizes are:[9]

Alabama—$1 per $5 of loans not exceeding $75; 3–2 per cent at $200 to $300

Maryland—3 per cent to $300

Wisconsin—2½–2 per cent at $100; 1 per cent at $200 to $300

The high gross income ratio in Alabama is due to the unusually high rate ceiling permitted on loans up $75 and the high proportion of loans made at this very small size. Such loans are very expensive to make and are usually made to high-risk borrowers; they would not be profitable under the rates permitted under most other small-loan statutes. The rate permitted on loans under $75 illustrates the dilemma faced by legislators. Is it better to legalize rates widely regarded as unconscionable and exercise control of harassment and harsh collection practices of lenders licensed under the statute, or is it better to set lower rate ceilings and enforce the denial of credit to those who cannot qualify by enforcing sanctions against loan sharks? Such decisions rest properly with legislative authorities familiar with local conditions relating to the urgency of need and demand for small loans. In 1964, some 71 per cent of the number of loans made and 26 per cent of the amount of loans were less than $75 in Alabama.[10] That the loan ceiling is low ($300) and the demand for very small, risky loans is high means that Alabama leads the states in the sample in gross income,

[9] The method of expressing graduated rates as noted below is common. Using Wisconsin as an example, 2½ per cent per month is the rate applied on outstanding balances up to $100, 2 per cent per month on that portion of the outstanding balance between $100 and $200, and 1 per cent per month on the portion between $200 and $300. See Appendix 2 for a compilation of ceiling rates, loan ceilings, and other state regulations.

[10] An interesting comparison of the effect of alternative rate ceilings upon the distribution of loans made in two $300-ceiling states reveals that a state with a flat rate (Maryland) made most of its loans in the largest loan size group.

	Percentage of Number		Percentage of Amount	
	Ala.	Md.	Ala.	Md.
$75 or less	71	—	26	—
$100 or less	—	15	—	5
$76–$200	12	—	19	—
$100 to $200	—	26	—	20
$200 to $300	17	59	55	75
	100%	100%	100%	100%

operating expense, and bad-debt ratios, along with the smallest average size of loan. Yet is is notable that Alabama does not lead in the highest net operating income ratio. In fact, Alabama's net operating income ratio, $7.90, is below the average of $9.06 per hundred of average loans outstanding for the thirty states.

Wisconsin provides an interesting contrast to Alabama in the $300 loan ceiling group (see Table 22, below). Its rate ceilings are low relative to both Alabama and Maryland. Confined to relatively low rates for loans $300 and under, licensed lenders must curtail expense ratios and risks to earn the lowest net operating income ratio of $4.30 per hundred among the thirty states. There are two reasons why firms may be willing to supply small loans in Wisconsin: they are allowed, first, to purchase sales finance paper and, second, to make both small (under $300) and larger loans under a different section of the statute from that regulating small loans. Under these conditions, one would not expect the population to be well served with loans under the small-loan law because there is little incentive to provide small loans. Table 30, below, reveals that Wisconsin has by far the highest ratio of population to the average number of statutory small loans outstanding, 88.2, more than triple the ratio of any of the twenty-nine other states. It is evident that the provisions of the Wisconsin Small Loan Law do not encourage small loans under that act.

It is not surprising that the very small average loan sizes attained in states with $300 loan ceilings result in extremes of high gross income, high operating expense, high risk, and low net operating income per dollar of average loans outstanding. The low loan ceiling limit necessitates high servicing costs per dollar of loan balance because investigation and bookkeeping costs remain relatively the same for loans of all sizes. Furthermore, people who can only qualify for loans in small amounts are likely to have low or unstable incomes, giving these loans a high risk. Such borrowers often borrow from more than one lender to evade loan limits. Thus rates must be high, producing high gross income ratios to match the high expense ratios per dollar of loans outstanding. Political problems, particularly inherent in the definition of what is usury, prevent states from setting rates on very small loans which offer a net operating income consistent with that earned on larger-sized loans. Fundamentally, the question boils down to whether individuals who can only qualify for loans in small amounts should be allowed to borrow at all. Practically, as the history of small loan legislation suggests, the real question is whether these individuals borrow from legal lenders under regulated conditions or from illegal sources, with the consequent abuses and harassment which abound under unregulated conditions.[11]

New York is the state with the lowest gross income and operating expense ratios per dollar of loans outstanding. As in other cases, it is the combination of the rate structure which, in conjunction with the size distribution of loans, determines the gross income ratio.[12] New York's rate structure is 2½–2 per cent at $100, ¾ per cent at $300 to $800. In each loan bracket, the ceiling rate of charge is low relative to those in other states, and the preponderance of loans (58 per cent) made in the largest loan bracket ensures a low gross income ratio. New York's expense ratio per $100 of average loans outstanding ($10.70) includes a low bad-debt ratio ($2.00) and accompanies the largest number of loans per office (1,697) of any of the thirty states.[13] Although both gross income and expense ratios per $100 of average loans outstanding decline with average loan size among all thirty states, New York's $440 average loan size ranks only twelfth largest. Thus it appears that high utilization of offices and low acceptance of risk overcome low rate ceilings to achieve a net operating income ratio of $9.50 in New York, somewhat higher than average among the thirty states. Yet it is significant that the ratio of New York's population to the average number of loans outstanding is relatively high. Using the reciprocal of this ratio, New York ranks twenty-sixth among thirty states in the quantity of small-loan services provided to borrowers. Its licensing restrictions may contribute to inadequate coverage of the market; perhaps if they were eased, more offices would increase small loan services.[14]

West Virginia, also an $800 loan ceiling state, has the highest net operating income ratio of $12.40 per $100 of average loans outstanding. It has a higher rate ceiling structure than New York, 3–2 per cent per month at $200, and 1½ per cent at $600. This produces a high gross income ratio, which combines with a moderate expense ratio to produce the high net operating income ratio.

[11] For a thorough description of laws and business practices in states with inadequate laws, see William Hays Simpson, *America's Small Loan Problem,* published by the author in cooperation with the Division of General Studies and Extension, University of South Carolina, 1963.

[12] It should be recalled that income from insurance and other charges is also included in gross income along with recoveries of loans previously written off.

[13] New York was the fourth most densely populated state in 1934, ranking behind New Jersey, Massachusetts, and Connecticut. It also had licensing restrictions imposed by a tightly administered convenience and advantage clause.

[14] Further discussion of this point, based upon several states, will be included below.

The lowest bad-debt ratios are found in New Hampshire and New Jersey, at $1.70 per $100 of average loans outstanding, contrasting sharply with the average of $2.97 in all states and with Alabama's high ratio of $6.00. The latter is, of course, the result of the high-risk loans under $75.00 made in Alabama. Both New Hampshire and New Jersey have relatively low gross income and bad-debt ratios, given their average loan sizes, which suggests that risk acceptance is lowered with lower rates charged.

This review of the average of operating income and cost ratios has suggested various characteristics of the regulated small-loan industry as it exists among the thirty states considered. First, there is considerable diversity in the operating ratios among the states. Second, by considering the states represented at the extremes of the range of high and low ratios, we have been able to note that the rate structures, in conjunction with different distributions of loans made, produce variations in gross income accompanied by variations in operating expenses, average loan sizes, bad debts, and net operating income. In some states, relatively high gross income ratios appear to be the main reason for high net operating income ratios. In others, expense ratios appeared to contribute to differences in net operating income. We turn now to a further clarification of these relationships among all thirty states.

Operating Ratios in Regulated Small-Loan Markets

In unregulated markets, one would expect that a higher rate of charge would permit the assumption of greater risk, which, in turn, might be rewarded by higher profit.[15] In regulated small-loan markets, rate ceilings and ceilings on size of loan govern the ratio of gross income to average loans outstanding because licensees normally charge borrowers the ceiling rate. Since most rate ceilings graduate the rate downward in brackets or intervals on the portions of a loan above the first bracket, the distribution of loans made and outstanding will often reflect an incentive implied by the slope of the rate ceiling structure in relation to expenses. Thus, although lenders have little incentive to charge below-ceiling rates, they may have some incentive to accept loans of a certain size which, in turn, will make the gross income ratio

[15] In addition to the statutory ceilings noted, the kinds of legal remedies provided creditors to collect indebtedness affect their willingness to assume risk.

per $100 of average loans outstanding different from the gross income ratio in another state. If operating expense ratios drop more rapidly than gross income ratios as average loan size rises, lenders will have greater incentive to make larger loans and maintain larger average loan sizes. Conversely, when the operating expense ratio drops less rapidly than the gross income ratio, there is less incentive to make and maintain larger average loan sizes. Finally, if there is little future possibility of making a gross income adequate to cover expenses and return a sufficient net operating income to provide a competitive return on capital, small-loan activity will decline.

In regulated small-loan markets of thirty states, we analyze the simple associations between ratios selected to give us insights into whether legal limitations upon rates of charge, loan ceilings, the number of offices, and other factors affect the profitability of operations and the risks assumed by consumer finance companies under the small-loan laws.

We turn our attention, first, to gross income ratios; second, to operating expense ratios; and third, to net operating income ratios. The actual ratios are reproduced in Table 22, grouped according to small-loan ceilings enacted by the states.

Gross Income Ratios per $100 of Average Loans Outstanding and per Loan Account

The graduated rate ceilings of many states are designed so that the higher rate ceilings in the smaller loan brackets are too low to cover expenses and return a normal profit.[16]

[16] Eight of the thirty states enacted rate ceilings on loans of $300 and under which are 2½ per cent per month or less. The states are Massachusetts, Michigan, Missouri, Nebraska, New Jersey, New York, North Dakota, Virginia, and Wisconsin.

For example, in New York, the rate ceilings on loans up to $300 (2½–2 at $100) have been justified by the Banking Department as follows: "Support for elevating or stretching the rate at the lower end of the loan range derives from the well-known fact that new loan writings of $300 or less tend to be unprofitable. Inferentially, an increase would encourage more smaller loans since a 'realistic' return would then be had. Were this solely a matter of encouraging the smaller loans, there would be much to be said for this viewpoint.

"It is, however, doubtful whether relief at the lower end of the loan range would encourage more lending in the smallest category. For these small loans to pay their way, the rate required would have to be far more than 3 per cent. In-

Yet if licensees are expected to meet the demand for these loans, they must obtain more favorable returns on larger loans in order to earn a competitive return on all loans. The political difficulty in legislating rate ceilings on smaller loans applies especially to those states with low loan ceilings. States with $300 loan ceilings may encounter problems, as we have seen, in setting high enough rates to earn a competitive average return on capital. Table 23 shows gross income ratios per $100 of average loans outstanding among the thirty states are negatively correlated with the size of average loan, thus supporting the proposition that rates are graduated downward among the states as average loan sizes are larger. The weaker correlation between the same gross income ratios and loan ceilings suggests that average loan size is not highly correlated with loan ceilings but perhaps with the incentives which rate ceilings provide in relation to expenses. In Table 22 one can also note that average loan sizes tend to rise with loan ceilings until the ceiling limit rises above $2,000. Above that amount, there is little tendency for average loan sizes to be higher, but gross income ratios still tend to be higher or lower more or less according to the average loan size.

More important is the association between the bad-debt ratio and the gross-income ratios shown in Table 23. It reveals a strong positive association which allows us to say that higher rates of gross income are accompanied by higher risks, under the assumption that bad-debt ratios reflect differences in the creditworthiness of borrowers accepted for loans. Yet the correlation between the gross and net income ratios (per $100 of average loans outstanding) is only —.12, which is not strong enough to suggest that higher rates and higher risks have any association with higher or lower profits. On this basis, observed differences in small-loan markets between states support the reasoning that higher average rates of gross income do accompany higher average assumption of risk without any apparent effect on the observed measure of profit.

The positive association between gross income per loan account and net operating income per $100 of average loans outstanding (.54) is of interest, especially in view of the low correlation between the gross-income ratio per dollar of loans outstanding and net operating income. Since the relation between gross income per loan account and gross income per dollar of loans outstanding is purely a function of

---

deed, it would be so high as to make it socially undesirable. . . ." *An Analysis of the Licensed Lender Industry, New York State, 1945–57,* New York State Banking Department, 1957, p. 57.

TABLE 22

Selected Operating Ratios in Thirty States, 1964

States in Loan Ceiling Groups[a]	Gross Income	Operating Expense	Net Operating Income	Bad Debts	Average Loan Size ($)	Gross Income	Operating Expense	Net Operating Income
	(Dollars per $100 of Average Loans Outstanding)					(Dollars per Loan Account)		
$300 Ceiling								
Alabama	40.70	32.80	7.90	6.00	131	53.19	42.82	10.37
Maryland	32.40	23.20	9.20	4.30	203	65.82	47.11	18.71
Wisconsin	27.10	22.80	4.30	3.90	160	43.23	36.30	6.94
$500 Ceiling								
Iowa[b]	27.30	19.40	7.90	2.40	286	78.00	55.51	22.49
New Jersey	22.90	13.60	9.30	1.70	337	77.36	45.86	31.50
$600 Ceiling								
Minnesota	29.70	20.10	9.60	3.90	324	96.07	64.97	31.10
Florida	28.40	18.60	9.80	3.80	366	103.91	68.18	35.73
Virginia	25.40	14.30	11.10	2.50	347	88.25	49.81	38.44
Pennsylvania	23.40	14.60	8.80	2.30	348	81.47	50.75	30.72
$800 Ceiling								
West Virginia	28.60	16.20	12.40	2.60	400	114.50	64.90	49.60
Kentucky	26.40	17.40	9.00	3.40	392	103.55	68.20	35.35
Illinois	24.10	16.00	8.10	3.20	391	94.11	62.44	31.67
New York	20.20	10.70	9.50	2.00	440	88.88	46.99	42.01

$1,000 Ceiling								
Arizona	29.10	20.90	8.20	5.00	372	108.22	77.86	30.36
Washington	26.70	16.00	10.70	2.80	448	119.62	71.59	48.03
N. Dakota	25.40	15.60	9.80	2.10	428	108.76	66.83	41.93
New Mexico	24.70	15.60	9.10	2.80	440	108.86	68.52	40.33
Indiana	24.60	15.00	9.60	2.60	447	109.90	67.04	42.86
Connecticut[b]	22.20	12.20	10.00	2.30	474	104.89	57.71	47.18
Michigan	22.00	12.80	9.20	2.10	484	106.71	61.90	44.81
$1,500 Ceiling								
Oregon	24.40	16.00	8.40	3.40	513	125.32	82.02	43.30
N. Hampshire	21.20	12.10	9.10	1.70	530	112.17	64.24	47.93
$2,000 Ceiling								
Ohio	20.80	11.00	9.80	1.90	588	122.25	64.45	57.79
$2,100 Ceiling								
Kansas	21.40	12.90	8.50	2.40	499	106.70	64.49	42.21
$2,500 Ceiling								
Georgia	27.00	18.90	8.10	3.30	361	97.54	68.37	29.17
Maine	25.40	14.50	10.90	3.00	448	113.99	65.01	48.98
Nevada	23.80	16.40	7.40	3.80	470	111.74	76.89	34.85
$3,000 Ceiling								
Massachusetts	23.40	11.80	11.60	2.00	495	115.61	58.68	56.93
Nebraska	21.20	13.90	7.30	2.20	506	107.43	70.28	37.15
No Ceiling								
S. Carolina	28.90	21.60	7.30	3.30	263	76.01	56.86	19.15

a Ranked within groups by height of gross-income ratio.
b Insurance income and expense not included in data.

TABLE 23

Simple Associations Between Gross Income Ratios and Selected
Ratios, Thirty States, 1964

	Simple Correlation Coefficients	
Selected Ratios[a]	Gross Income per $100 of Average Loans Outstanding	Gross Income per Loan Account
Bad debts	.84*	−.40*
Net operating income	−.12	.54*
Loans per office	−.27	−.04
Per capita income	−.50*	.11
Average loan size	−.79*	.90*
Loan ceilings	−.24	.30

[a] All operating income, expense, and bad-debt ratios are per $100 of average loans outstanding unless stated to the contrary.

* At the 5 per cent significance level, any correlation coefficient which is .37 or more is unlikely to have occurred by chance in a sample having thirty observations.

the size of average loan,[17] it would appear that the positive association between gross income per loan account and the net operating income ratio reflects a higher rate of net operating income as average loan size increases.

We are also interested in the extent to which differences in gross income ratios per $100 of average loans outstanding accompany differences in the number of loans per office among the states. The correlation of this measure with loans per office (−.27) is not strong enough to presume any relation between the two.

When states have higher per capita incomes, the gross-income ratios per $100 of average loan outstanding tend to be lower (−.50, Table 23). States with higher per capita incomes tend to have higher average loan sizes, lower average risks, and lower gross income ratios.

Operating Expense Ratios per $100 of Average Loans Outstanding and per Loan Account

Differences in operating expense ratios accompany differences in gross-income ratios and help determine the degree to which small-loan borrowers can be served in any state. As was the case with the gross-income ratios, expense ratios per $100 of average loans outstand-

[17] Gross income per loan account divided by average loan size times 100 equals gross income per dollar of average loans outstanding.

TABLE 24
Simple Associations Between Operating Expense Ratios
and Selected Ratios, Thirty States, 1964

	Simple Correlation Coefficients	
Selected Ratios[a]	Operating Expense per $100 of Average Loans Outstanding	Operating Expense per Loan Account
Bad debts[b]	.88*	−.01
Loans per office	−.38*	−.32
Per capita income	−.46*	−.07
Average loan size	−.85*	.64*
Loan ceiling	−.18	.32

Note: Operating expense ratios are before interest and income taxes.

[a] All operating income, expense, and bad-debt ratios are per $100 of average loans outstanding unless stated to the contrary.

[b] Since bad debts are part of operating expense, the correlation is enlarged accordingly. The simple correlation between the bad-debt ratios and the operating expense less bad-debt ratios per $100 of average loans outstanding is .82.*

* Statistically significant. See note to Table 23.

ing decline with average loan size and rise per loan account (see Table 24). The associations are much weaker with loan ceilings, for the same reasons noted in the previous section. Both gross income and operating expense ratios tend to have similar associations with average loan size, and loan ceiling.

Operating expense ratios are positively correlated with bad-debt ratios, even when the two ratios are correlated after bad debts have been removed from operating expenses. This implies that higher risks require higher operating expenses other than that portion involved in provision for loss. The reason is that investigation and collection effort must be intensified when dealing with higher-risk loans.

The major finding which emerges from correlating expense ratios with the ratios shown in Table 24 is that the average number of loans per office is negatively associated with operating expense ratios (−.38 and −.32) both per $100 of average loans outstanding and per loan account. Thus, an important method of lowering expense is to increase the number of loans per office. In some cases this may be done by locating offices in areas of high population density, provided that the number of loan offices already serving customers is not already too large to promise high loan per office ratios. It is here that restriction of entry through convenience and advantage clauses giving the state

TABLE 25
Simple Associations Between Net Operating Income
Ratios and Selected Ratios, Thirty States, 1964

| | Simple Correlation Coefficients | |
Selected Ratios	Net Operating Income per $100 of Average Loans Outstanding	Net Operating Income per Loan Account
Operating expense[a]	− .44*	.18
Bad debts[a]	− .37*	− .65*
Loans per office	.41*	.21
Per capita income	.03	.24
Average loan size	.40*	.91*
Loan ceiling	− .09	.20

Note: Net operating income ratios are before interest and income taxes.
[a] Per $100 of average loans outstanding.
* Statistically significant. See note to Table 23.

loan supervisor power to approve new offices is strategic. Through this device loans per office can be higher and expense ratios lower. Whether or not net operating income will be higher depends upon whether the rate structure permitted in the state offsets the economies permitted by restriction of entry.

Net Operating Income Ratios

Table 25 reveals that net operating income ratios per $100 of average loans outstanding were higher when operating expense ratios were lower, suggesting that achieving lower expense ratios is the major means to higher operating profitability.[18] Lower bad-debt ratios are a means of doing this since they are associated with higher net operating income ratios both per $100 of average loans outstanding and per loan account. While it remains true that licensees are more selective in making larger loans than smaller ones, the fact that bad debts per $100 of average loans outstanding are negatively correlated with net operating income ratios confirms the common notion that it is also more profitable to curtail risk for a given loan size.

[18] The correlation coefficient was slightly larger (−.46) for the seventeen states with no other loan laws permitting consumer finance company operations.

Since increasing loans per office is apparently a successful means of lowering expenses, it may also accompany higher net operating income ratios per $100 of average loans outstanding, indicated by the .41 correlation in Table 25. Yet the relation is influenced by the inclusion of the thirteen states whose expenses include allocations based on operations under more than one law. For the seventeen states without other loan laws the correlation was .28, which is somewhat weaker, and well below any acceptable significance level.[19]

It is of interest to note that larger average loan sizes are associated with higher net operating income ratios, but this result also is not significant among the seventeen states where operations are confined to the small-loan law. There is no positive association between higher ceilings and higher net operating income ratios in Table 25. It has already been pointed out that average loan sizes do not appear to rise with higher ceilings above $2,000, and the correlation between average size of loan and loan ceilings (.33) indicates that the presence of a higher loan ceiling does not necessarily imply a larger average size of loan or higher operating profitability.[20]

The conclusion to be drawn from these data with respect to operating profitability is that small-loan licensees appear to be able to adjust expense and income ratios by regulating their average loan sizes and risks assumed according to the opportunities presented under statutory regulation. It has been noted that operating expenses and risks assumed vary directly with the gross income ratio, which results, primarily, from opportunities presented by the rate structure and loan ceilings set in the statute. Operating profits result from income-expense relationships which, between states, appear to be related to the degree of risk assumed, and the number of offices in relation to the population.

Measuring Loan Services Under the Small-Loan Laws: Presence of Other Laws

Any measure of loan services provided under small-loan statutes is critical because it often accompanies judgments about the "adequacy"

---

[19] The standard of acceptability used here, the 5 per cent significance level, implies odds of 19 to 1 that the result may have occurred through chance. For the coefficient of .28 in seventeen states, the odds are only about 3 to 1.

[20] It is likely that competition for larger loans from other institutions, in addition to the level of rate ceilings, affects the average size of loan under small-loan statutes with ceilings above $2,000.

or "inadequacy" of legislation in a highly regulated industry. But these judgments can be made only in terms of legislation whose objectives, in the case of small loans, were to permit a regulated small-loan industry to replace the abuses of unregulated lending by:

1) Authorizing rates of charge sufficient to permit profitable operation by legitimate capital,
2) requiring those who charge such rates to submit to restraints for the borrower's protection, and
3) eliminating lenders who will not conform to regulation.[21]

If the objectives of legislation were to maximize the quantity of loan services to borrowers, one would not limit the rate of charge and size of loan by law, since an unregulated market would probably best achieve that goal. Yet the enlargement of the quantity of legal loan services is the implicit goal of the first objective quoted above, although it must be accompanied by protection of the borrower and elimination of illegal lenders. Clearly, the more profitable are operations under law, the less is the problem of effective enforcement of illegal operations since a wider flow of loans is legally available. At the same time there is less protection from higher rates. For our purposes we regard population per loan and per capita loans outstanding as alternative measures of the quantity of loan services provided. Either tests the different regulatory philosophies which exist among the states under existing laws. The first provides only a rough measure of the number of borrowers served because of multiple loans. The second measures the amount of funds utilized proportionately to the population in a state. Since the ranges of population per loan and per capita loans outstanding are wide among the thirty states, those states at the extremes may well wish to compare their performance with their objectives relative to other states. Since differences in loan ceilings imposed imply different definitions of what constitutes a regulated small loan, these differences are attributable to regulatory philosophy as well. In this chapter we make no attempt to evaluate regulatory philosophies among the states. We do, however, seek to point out the differences in the quantities of small-loan services which accompany different regulatory philosophies.

Population per loan ratios have been ranked inversely, from low to high, in Table 26 so that higher rankings reflect a greater number of loans per capita in a state. Per capita loans outstanding are ranked

[21] F. B. Hubacheck, "The Development of Regulatory Small Loan Laws," *Law and Contemporary Problems*, Winter, 1941, p. 109.

from high to low to measure the declining per capita provision of dollars under the small-loan laws of the states. Finally, we identify thirteen states with supplementary (larger loan) laws which permit consumer finance companies to make other loans than those counted here. Such loans are often not larger than those allowed under small-loan statutes in other states with higher statutory loan ceilings. We consider the impact of other loan laws upon the two measures of loan service in this section, but make no attempt to measure the provision of loan services under other loan laws because the data are not available for small-loan licensees only and the loans are often made under regulatory conditions which differ markedly in protective features from those under the small-loan laws.[22]

In Table 26, the two states which provide the largest amount of loan services (lowest population per loan ratios), Georgia and South Carolina, both have unusual regulatory features with respect to rate of charge. Neither state follows the principle of the all-inclusive charge contained in the uniform-small-loan-law drafts and both laws allow fees in addition to the rate. Their maximum rate and loan sizes in 1964 are as follows:

Georgia	*South Carolina*
8 per cent a year to $2,500 discount for eighteen months, add-on for longer maturities; fee of 8 per cent of the first $600 and 4 per cent of the excess	Initial charge, 6 per cent of each cash advance plus 6 per cent per annum add-on to $200; $1.75 per month expense fee on loans $100 or over, 7 per cent per annum on portion over $200, no maxmium loan size

The fees permitted in both states raise the effective rate of charge on smaller loans, especially in South Carolina, where the fee is a fixed dollar amount multiplied by the number of months. Both are relatively low-income states where the demand for smaller loans tends to be

[22] The protective features cited are those recommended in various drafts of the Uniform Small Loan Law and enacted in a majority of the thirty states. They include the principle of an all-inclusive charge for loans, prepayment at the option of the borrower with rebates determined under specified conditions, a uniform system of disclosing charges, and specification of the form and content of the loan agreement. In addition there are a few states, i.e., New Hampshire, where consumer finance companies make loans under the General Interest (usury) Laws when the height of the usury rate ceiling does not impair profitable operations. Such statutes offer little or no regulatory protection to the borrower.

TABLE 26

Ranking of States Under Alternative Measures of the Provision of Small-Loan Services and Related Statutory Provisions

States (ranked low to high by population per loan)	Population per Loan	Per Capita Loans Outstanding ($)	Ranking (high to low)	Population per Office Ranking (high to low)	Other Loan Law	Small-Loan Ceiling ($)	Average Loan Size ($)
1. Georgia	6.2	58.53	1	29	no	2,500	361
2. South Carolina	7.4	35.64	11	30	no	none	263
3. New Mexico	8.8	49.75	2	28	no	1,000	440
4. Florida	9.81	37.30	10	24	no	600	366
5. Kentucky	9.83	39.91	8	19	yes	800	392
6. Indiana	10.6	42.12	5	25	yes	1,000	447
7. Nevada	11.1	42.43	4	18	no	2,500	470
8. Ohio	12.0	48.90	3	21	no	2,000	588
9. Kansas	12.2	40.96	7	26	no	2,100	499
10. Alabama	12.3	10.62	29	20	yes	300	131
11. West Virginia	12.4	32.30	13	14	yes	800	400
12. Maryland	12.5	16.30	26	13	yes	300	203
13. New Hampshire	12.9	41.16	6	27	no[a]	1,500	530
14. Arizona	13.35	27.88	17	23	yes	1,000	372
15. Nebraska	13.43	37.68	9	22	no	3,000	506
16. Virginia	13.8	25.17	18	7	no	600	347

17. Pennsylvania	14.5	23.99	20	11	yes	600	348
18. Michigan	14.8	32.59	12	9	no	1,000	484
19. Maine	15.6	28.70	15	15	no	2,500	448
20. New Jersey	15.65	21.55	22	4	no	500	337
21. Illinois	15.7	24.88	19	10	yes	800	391
22. Oregon	16.8	30.57	14	17	yes	1,500	513
23. Massachusetts	17.6	28.16	16	6	no	3,000	495
24. Washington	19.4	23.03	21	8	yes	1,000	448
25. Iowa	20.8	13.77	27	16	yes	500	286
26. New York	21.1	20.82	23	1	no	800	440
27. Connecticut	24.7	19.19	24	2	no	1,000	474
28. North Dakota	25.8	16.56	25	12	no	1,000	428
29. Minnesota	28.8	11.24	28	3	yes	600	324
30. Wisconsin	88.2	1.81	30	5	yes	300	160
Average for 17 states with no other loan law	14.3	34.42				1,544[b]	440
Average for 13 states with other loan laws	21.2	22.96				731	340

[a] Loans larger than $1,500 are made under the General Interest (usury) Law, which has no rate ceiling.
[b] Excludes South Carolina, which has no loan ceiling.

large. Under the constant-ratio formula, the approximate rate of charge on a $100 loan for one year in Georgia is about 30 per cent; in South Carolina it is about 59 per cent. The rate for a $500 one-year loan in Georgia stays the same, whereas in South Carolina it drops to 30 per cent. Yet the gross income ratios per $100 of average loans outstanding are not unusually high in Georgia and South Carolina, 27.0 and 28.9, respectively. Nor are the net operating income ratios per $100 of average loan balance above average—8.1 and 7.3, respectively.

Whether the rate structures in these states are too high or too low cannot be settled on the basis of information available here. What is clear, however, is that the quantity of small-loan services provided borrowers in these states are the highest among the thirty states. Judged by our second measure of loan service, per capita loans outstanding, Georgia remains the highest-ranking state and South Carolina drops to eleventh because of its smaller average loan size.[23] It is interesting to note that the per capita income of each of the first five states ranked by population per loan is below the average for the thirty states. The demand for smaller loans could be expected to be stronger in states with lower per capita incomes because a larger proportion of potential borrowers need a lender of last resort.

When the states are ranked by per capita loans outstanding in Table 26, the rankings change, but not markedly.[24] Thus, differences in the two measures of loan service do not affect the rankings appreciably. The two states most affected are Maryland and Alabama, which both have a relatively small average loan size that gives them much lower ranking when per capita loans outstanding is the measure of loan services.

If regulatory philosophies are concerned with the proportion of borrowers in a state who receive small-loan services, population per loan is the better measure of that objective. If legislators want to measure the effectiveness of legislation in attracting capital, the per capita average of loans outstanding is the better measure. In states where average loan sizes are small, as in Alabama, Maryland, and South Carolina, both measures should be used to ensure that multiple loans do not give an illusion of greater loan service when population per loan is considered by itself.

The presence of other loan laws among the states appears to affect

[23] A large difference in ranking of population per loan and per capita loans outstanding suggests that multiple loans may be prevalent.

[24] When the rankings of population per loan and per capita loans outstanding are correlated, the rank correlation coefficient is .77.

the services provided under the small-loan law as indicated by the data of Table 26. None of the four states with the highest small-loan service rankings by either measure have other loan laws. Yet states like Kentucky, Indiana, and West Virginia achieve relatively high rankings despite the presence of other laws which permit consumer finance companies to operate under both. In these states, the terms of the other loan laws are not more favorable to profitable operations in the range of loan sizes covered by the small-loan law. On the other hand, there are states in the lower loan service rankings with other laws, which suggests that other statutes may provide the basis for more profitable operations. Wisconsin, Minnesota, Iowa, Washington, Oregon, Illinois, and Pennsylvania all have statutes which provide more favorable rate alternatives for larger loans than the states with higher small loan service rankings.

Among the states with no other loan laws and low loan service ranking, North Dakota, Connecticut, New York, Massachusetts, and New Jersey need to be mentioned. All but the first are states with tightly administered convenience and advantage clauses as indicated by high population to office ratios. North Dakota has a relatively high population to office ratio simply because it has the lowest proportion of urban population among the thirty states. Thus, while the presence of other loan laws may account for some of the states which provide relatively low quantities of loan service under the small-loan laws, we must look to other aspects of small-loan statutes to account for these states with low rankings.

On balance, it would appear that the presence of other loan laws has affected the provision of services under the small-loan laws. Table 26 compares the averages for the seventeen states with no other loan laws with those of the thirteen states having other laws permitting consumer finance company operations. Both the population per loan and per capita loans outstanding measures of loan service suggest that loan services provided under small-loan laws are appreciably less in states that have other loan laws than in those that do not have them. Some of the impact has come because states instead of raising loan ceilings have apparently regarded parallel operations under other laws as satisfying their needs. In a sense, this suggests that larger loan borrowers do not require the standards of protection normally present in a small-loan statute modeled on the principles of the uniform-small-loan law. The extent of the impact of other loan laws depends upon the relative attractiveness to the licensee of operating under one or the other statute. Thus, where the rate structure is highly restrictive, as in the case of Wisconsin's small-loan law,[25] a large impact results because operations under other loan laws are relatively more attractive. In other states, the rate structure may be relatively more attractive as regards the small-loan statute, but larger loans are made which could not be made under it.

Convenience and Advantage Clauses in Relation to Loan Service

Convenience and advantage clauses provide a means of increasing the number of loans per office by holding down the number of offices in relation to markets served. This tends to lower operating costs and, in the absence of offsetting factors, to increase net operating income. Yet comparing the twenty-four states with C and A clauses with the six states without clauses does not provide a good basis for measuring the regulatory use of the power to restrain entry; these powers are applied differently by the separate authorities. Nor is it desirable to measure restraint on entry in states allowing small-loan licensees to operate under other loan laws. An officer of one of the large national consumer finance companies was asked to classify states according to the severity with which these clauses were administered in 1964 in granting licenses for new offices. His response indicates that such a classification does imply effective restraint on entry on the basis of both measures of the provision of loan services.[26]

Table 27 compares the rankings of the seventeen states with no other loan laws according to population per office ratios (and C and A status) with ranking based on loans per office, population per loan, and per capita loans outstanding. The first six states fall within the six highest loans per office rankings and within the eight lowest when ranked by the provision of loan services under small-loan statutes. These comparisons imply that when convenience and advantage is tightly administered, the number of offices is not as large as it might

[25] Wisconsin is obviously a special case because the loan laws in that state permit licensees to operate under a discount loan law in addition to the small-loan statute. The number of loans under the discount loan law within the $300 limit permitted by the small-loan law represents 30 per cent of the number of loans made in 1964 under the two statutes. Since loans outstanding under other statutes are not included in the measures of small-loan services, Wisconsin's average number of loans per office, population per loan, and net operating income ratios rank the lowest among the thirty states.

[26] South Carolina is the major exception to this statement.

TABLE 27

Comparison of Seventeen States Ranked by Population per Office and Loans
per Office with Rankings by Loan Service Measures

| States with No Other Loan Laws,[a] Ranked by Population per Office (high to low) | Restraint of Entry Under Convenience and Advantage Clause[b] | Loans per Office Rank | Loan Service | |
			Population per Loan Rank (low to high)	Per Capita Loans Outstanding Rank (high to low)
1. New York	tight	1	14	15
2. Connecticut	tight	4	16	16
3. New Jersey	tight	2	13	14
4. Massachusetts	tight	5	15	12
5. Virginia	tight	3	10	13
6. Michigan	tight	6	11	10
7. North Dakota	none	17	17	17
8. Maine	none	11	12	11
9. Nevada	medium	7	5	4
10. Ohio	medium	10	6	3
11. Nebraska	medium	14	9	7
12. Florida	medium	9	4	8
13. Kansas	none	15	7	6
14. New Hampshire	none	16	8	5
15. New Mexico	medium	13	3	2
16. Georgia	slight	8	1	1
17. South Carolina	tight	12	2	9

[a] Under which small-loan licensees can operate (usury laws excepted).

[b] Subjective measure obtained from consumer finance company official.

otherwise be and the number of loans per office is correspondingly
higher. When the number of loans per office is high, operating expense ratios tend to be lower, but the loan service measures also tend
to be low. It is entirely possible, but not likely, that population density
alone could result in high loans per office ratios in the absence of convenience and advantage clauses in the statutes of the six states. The
reason that it is not likely is because the six states, for the most part,
have above-average net operating income ratios which would tend to
attract additional licensees. The evidence in Table 27 for the eleven
other states offers mixed support for the case that moderate restraint
of entry decreases the provision of loan services.

So while it is difficult to say that convenience and advantage
clauses result in higher population per office ratios, there is a strong

implication that tightly administered clauses which restrain entry do contribute to more loans per office and lower expense ratios. By so doing, however, they exert an adverse effect upon the amount of loan services provided under the small-loan law.

Supplementary Insights from the Operating Ratios of the Four Largest Consumer Finance Companies

The operations of the four largest consumer finance companies—Household Finance, Beneficial Finance Company, Seaboard Finance, and American Investment—provide insights into the comparative behavior of large companies in relation to all companies. The companies provided data that made it possible to extend state coverage and measure unallocated operating expenses in each state. They held about 30 per cent of the average amount of loans outstanding under small-loan statutes in twenty-nine of the thirty states in 1964.[27]

Comparative Operating Experience: Four Large Companies and All Companies

The behavior of the four large companies in different state regulatory environments may be ascertained by comparing selected operating ratios for the four-company licensed offices with those of all licensees under the small-loan laws as reported to supervisory authorities in thirty states.[28] Then it will be noted that modest changes in these ratios were brought about by enlarging the sample by six of the seven additional states.[29]

In Table 28 it is apparent that the four large companies had larger

[27] Maine was excluded from this comparison because the four-company data were for 1964 and the state report data were for 1963.

[28] The fact that the large company operating ratios are based on average monthly outstanding loans, while the all-company ratios are the average of beginning- and end-of-year outstanding loans, lowers the denominator of the four-company ratios by an estimated 1½ to 2 per cent relative to the all-company ratios. The difference does not seriously impair the comparisons.

[29] The data for Oklahoma were not included in the averages for the larger sample shown here because the four companies experienced an average net operating loss under the small-loan statute in this state in 1964. The state was included in the other data used in this section, however.

TABLE 28
Comparative Operating Income and Cost Data for Licensed
Consumer Finance Offices, 1964

	Arithmetic Mean ($)		Coefficient of Variation (%)	
Ratios	Four Large Companies	All Companies	Four Large Companies	All Companies
Gross income per $100 of average loans outstanding				
30 states	24.97	25.63	11	16
36 states[a]	25.16	—	13	—
Operating expense per $100 of average loans outstanding				
30 states	14.69	16.56	25	28
36 states	15.37	—	30	—
Net operating income per $100 of average loans outstanding[b]				
30 states	10.28	9.06	22	17
36 states	9.77	—	25	—
Bad debts per $100 of average loans outstanding[c]				
30 states	2.60	2.96	38	34
36 states	2.66	—	38	—
Average loan size				
30 states	425	396	24	27
36 states	415	—	28	—

Note: Calendar years except for New Hampshire, North Dakota, and West Virginia.

[a] The thirty states plus California, Colorado, Louisiana, Missouri, North Carolina, and Rhode Island. A thirty-seventh state, Oklahoma, was omitted because of the effect of an average net operating loss upon the data.

[b] Before interest and taxes.

[c] Represented by either provision for losses or losses charged off.

average loans outstanding, lower gross income and operating expense ratios, and higher net operating income ratios, than did other licensed lenders in the thirty states. Their larger average size of loans is reflected by the lower gross income and operating expense ratios.

The lower bad-debt ratio accompanying the larger average size of loans implies a lower average risk acceptance, unless collection procedures of the large companies are more efficient than those of other companies. Finally, the four companies received a larger net operating income per $100 of average loans outstanding than their competitors.

These differences in operating ratios suggest that the large companies keep more of their dollars at work among the larger-loan, lower-risk borrowers than the other companies do. If the direction, plus or minus, of the difference in average size of loans is used as the basis for comparison within each state, the four-company average loan size was above that of all licensees in twenty-three of the thirty states.[30] Further, bad-debt ratios for the four companies were below those of all licensees in twenty-five of the thirty states.

The lesser variation in the gross income, operating expense, and average size of loans ratios for the four large companies in Table 28 suggests some greater standardization of their operations than occurs generally under the small-loan laws. This, however, is not the case with either the net operating income ratio or the bad-debt ratio. Thus, much of the variation in gross income and operating expense would appear to reflect differences in the average size of loans rather than differences in risks or profitability.

The addition of six states to the previous thirty results in only a moderate difference in the averages. On balance, operating expense ratios were raised more than gross income ratios, resulting in lower net operating income ratios on average. Bad-debt ratios were raised and average size of loans lowered. The coefficients of variation were enlarged for all of the ratios except the bad-debt ratio.

The higher net operating income ratios for the four large companies will require further investigation. With operations in virtually all of the states, these companies can adjust the scale of their operations within any state more easily than companies whose lending activities are confined to one or a relatively few states. It would be expected that the national companies would invest a larger proportion of their funds in those states where their profit opportunities are larger and where, if successful, they will obtain a larger share of the market. The rank correlations suggest that this may be the case. Table 29

---

[30] In this instance correction of the different bases for computing average loans outstanding would lower the four-company figure relative to the all-company figure since average loans outstanding is divided by the average number of loans to obtain average loan size. See footnote 27.

TABLE 29

Rank Correlations of Selected Ratios of Four Large Consumer
Finance Companies, Twenty-Nine States, 1964

Ratios Correlated[a]	Spearman's Rank Correlation Coefficient
Adjusted[b] net operating income per $100 of average monthly loans outstanding and	.46*
Average monthly loans outstanding in state	
Average monthly loans outstanding in 29 states	
Adjusted[b] net operating income per $100 of average monthly loans outstanding and	.38*
Four companies' average monthly loans outstanding in state	
All licensees' average loans outstanding in state[c]	
Number of loans per office for all licensees and	.62*
Average monthly loans outstanding in state	
Average monthly loans outstanding in 29 states	
Number of loans per office for all licensees and	.35*
Four companies' average monthly loans outstanding in state	
All licensees' average monthly loans outstanding in state[c]	

Note: Maine was not included in these correlations. See text note 26.

[a] All ratios are four-company ratios unless stated otherwise. The average monthly loans outstanding are averages computed from dollar amounts for the four companies added together. Each of the adjusted net operating income ratios is the simple average of the ratios for each company.

[b] The adjustment results from the subtraction of home office and regional office expense from operating expense.

[c] Average of beginning and end of year.

* Significance at the 5 per cent level as indicated by a coefficient of .31 or larger in a sample with twenty-nine observations; see Sidney Siegel, *Nonparametric Statistics*, New York, 1956, Table P, p. 284.

shows that the adjusted net operating income ratio[31] of the four companies is positively correlated, .46, with the proportion of the total four-company average monthly loans outstanding invested within the state. Further, the market share in the state represented by the ratio

[31] Net operating income before interest and taxes and before allocated regional office and home office expense was used to remove the influence of allocated expenses on the rankings.

of average (monthly) loans outstanding of the four companies to the average (beginning and end of year) loans outstanding for all licensees also was positively correlated, .38, with the adjusted net operating income of the four companies.

It is apparent that the national companies allocate larger portions of their invested funds to those states where the number of loans per office is high, as indicated by the .62 rank correlation coefficient in Table 29. This tendency may result in a larger market share, as suggested by a positive rank correlation of .35 between the average number of loans per office in the state and the share of average loans outstanding held by the four national companies.

The main insight into small-loan markets gained in this section is that the four large companies emphasize larger loans under the small-loan statutes more than the smaller companies do. Since these companies typically make loans in most states with effective small-loan laws, it is noteworthy that their capital was found to gravitate in directions where both profitability and loan service can be served jointly. To a large extent, this type of competitive adjustment to regulatory constraints is a normal part of any industry, especially one so highly regulated and supervised as is the small-loan industry today. Given the general objectives of curbing the abuses of unregulated lending and maintaining sufficient incentives under regulation to attract private capital, the wide disparity in loan services provided under the small-loan laws implies that greater uniformity in objectives and features of regulatory policies governing the small-loan industry would bring about both a more consistent regulatory atmosphere and more uniform protection to an enlarged group of borrowers under small-loan statutes.

Selected ratios, compiled from thirty state reports, are shown for each state in Table 30.

TABLE 30

Selected Ratios from Data in State Reports, Thirty States, 1964

States	Average Loans Outstanding (thous. $)	Average No. of Loans per Office	Population per Office	Rank High to Low	Population per Loan	Rank Low to High	Per Capita Income	Ratio of Urban to Total Population	Total Population (thous.)	Per Capita Loans Outstanding	Rank High to Low
Alabama	36,193	606	7,455	20	12.3	10	$1640	55	3,407	10.62	29
Arizona	44,082	491	6,560	23	13.4	14	2203	74	1,581	27.88	17
Connecticut	53,085	950	23,441	2	24.7	27	3127	78	2,766	19.19	24
Florida	212,770	648	6,360	24	9.8	4	2157	74	5,705	37.30	10
Georgia	251,332	665	4,101	29	6.2	1	1829	55	4,294	58.53	1
Illinois	261,020	768	12,056	10	15.7	21	2892	81	10,489	24.88	19
Indiana	203,230	593	6,299	25	10.6	6	2437	62	4,825	42.12	5
Iowa	37,948	417	8,664	16	20.8	25	2323	53	2,755	13.77	27
Kansas	91,130	513	6,250	26	12.2	9	2263	61	2,225	40.96	7
Kentucky	126,078	778	7,649	19	9.8	5	1774	44	3,159	39.91	8
Maine[a]	28,383	592	8,675	15	15.6	19	1999	51	989	28.70	15
Maryland	55,936	762	9,377	13	12.5	12	2734	73	3,432	16.30	26
Mass.	150,334	894	15,700	6	17.6	23	2811	84	5,338	28.16	16
Michigan	263,917	860	12,773	9	14.8	18	2568	73	8,098	32.59	12
Minnesota	39,568	799	23,013	3	28.8	29	2334	62	3,521	11.24	28
Nebraska	55,760	537	7,220	22	13.4	15	2300	54	1,480	37.68	9
Nevada	17,311	723	8,000	18	11.1	7	3203	70	408	42.43	4
New Hampshire[b]	26,921	462	5,945	27	12.9	13	2252	58	654	41.16	6
New Jersey	143,989	1414	22,126	4	15.7	20	2878	89	6,682	21.55	22
New Mexico	50,147	548	4,846	28	8.8	3	1981	66	1,008	49.75	2
New York	372,932	1697	35,758	1	21.1	26	3015	85	17,915	20.82	23
North Dakota[b]	10,678	402	10,403	12	25.8	28	2016	35	645	16.56	25

TABLE 30 (Continued)
Selected Ratios from Data in State Reports, Thirty States, 1964

States	Average Loans Out-standing (thous. $)	Average No. of Loans per Office	Popula-tion per Office	Rank High to Low	Popula-tion per Loan	Rank Low to High	Per Capita Income	Ratio of Urban to Total Popula-tion	Total Popula-tion (thous.)	Per Capita Loans Out-standing	Rank High to Low
Ohio	493,843	635	7,367	21	12.0	8	2516	73	10,100	48.90	3
Oregon	57,196	521	8,622	17	16.8	22	2467	62	1,871	30.57	14
Penna.	274,894	822	11,912	11	14.5	17	2452	72	11,459	23.99	20
So. Carolina	91,071	552	3,992	30	7.4	2	1575	41	2,555	35.64	11
Virginia	112,696	1104	15,231	7	13.8	16	2080	56	4,478	25.17	18
Washington	68,736	698	13,030	8	19.4	24	2558	68	2,984	23.03	21
West Virginia[b]	58,047	700	8,681	14	12.4	11	1847	38	1,797	32.30	13
Wisconsin	7,427	189	16,428	5	88.2	30	2365	64	4,107	1.81	30

[a] The figures for Maine are for 1963.
[b] Fiscal year.

V

Factors Affecting the Cost of Borrowing
by Consumer Finance Companies

JACK ZWICK

Graduate School of Business,
Columbia University

Chapter III dealt with the factors affecting operating costs and gross income during 1962–64 for a sample of forty-eight consumer finance companies. This chapter, using the same body of data, examines the factors influencing a most important component of "nonoperating" costs, namely, the cost of borrowed funds. As in Chapter III, the investigation here is based on average 1962–64 figures for each sample company. The first section of the chapter examines the nominal cost of borrowing for the sample by size of company. The sections following attempt to explain observed cost of borrowing differentials among the sample companies: first, differences in the degree of leverage are analyzed; second, discussion focuses on variations among the sample companies in the composition of liabilities.

The aggregate demands made by the consumer finance companies upon the capital markets are determined in volume by growth of aggregate receivables. The spectacular growth in demand for funds by the consumer finance industry over time was shown in Chapter I, which sketched the industry's history. It is interesting to note here that the external demands for funds are characterized by large proportions of debt in relation to equity.[1]

[1] Equity financing consists of both common stock and preferred stock issuances.

In contrast to the fractional debt ratios typical of most non-financial companies, the consumer finance companies obtain senior debt several times the size of their "risk-bearing base."[2] It is not uncommon for a consumer finance company to support $2.50 to $3.00 of senior debt with a $1 risk-bearing base. These multiple ratios are made feasible by the low "risk" in cash flows from the consumer finance company receivables. Stability in cash flows derives from low loss rates, diversity of risks, and large numbers of customers.[3] This type of security—i.e., receivables—is also common to the asset structures of sales finance companies and captive finance companies, and, of course, is the basis for the similarity of their claim structures. Diversification, or lack of it, plays a role in limiting the debt-equity proportions of the consumer finance companies.

The Cost of Borrowed Funds

As in the investigation of factors affecting operating costs and gross income, certain a priori notions existed regarding factors believed to be influential in accounting for differences in borrowing costs among the companies. First, it was presumed that borrowing costs would be lower for the larger companies because of their widespread access to the capital markets and money markets and excellent reputations among lenders. Second, once size of company has been taken into account, it seemed logical that borrowing costs would be higher for those companies characterized by high proportions of negotiated borrowings[4] to total assets; other things equal, the higher the degree of financial leverage, the greater the risk of default and, therefore, the higher the borrowing rate required to compensate lenders for the assumption of added risk. Third, the risk to lenders of extending credit to the sample companies is reflected to some extent in the respective companies' burden coverages; it was assumed that borrowing costs would be higher for those companies with comparatively low burden

[2] The risk-bearing base consists of common equity, preferred equity, junior subordinated debt, and senior subordinated debt.

[3] The most important dimension affecting variance of cash flows from a large portfolio of receivables is, of course, not the variance associated with the cash flows from individual loan accounts but rather the covariance between the flows from individual accounts and from the remainder of the portfolio.

[4] Negotiated borrowings, as distinct from total borrowings, exclude accruals and payables.

coverages.[5] Finally, it was anticipated that borrowing costs would vary with changes in asset composition—the riskier the asset composition, the higher the borrowing costs, other things equal.

Because a substantial degree of interrelationship was detected among the factors enumerated above, attempts to use the multiple regression technique to analyze the determinants of borrowing costs were not successful. Alternatively, simple regression coefficients were computed between each of the factors and borrowing costs. These tests suggested that differences in company size are more closely associated with variations in borrowing costs than are changes in any of the other factors.

Cost of Borrowing by Size of Company

Chart 19 portrays the relation between company size (expressed in logs of total assets to the base 10) and nominal borrowing costs (interest and debt amortization expenses divided by average negotiated borrowings outstanding). This statistically significant association between company size and nominal borrowing costs suggests that larger companies incur lower borrowing costs.[6]

In Table 31 the borrowing costs are broken down and averaged for six size categories.[7] The cost percentages increase without interruption as size category declines, thus supporting the conclusions implied

[5] Burden coverage is defined as EBIT (operating income before interest and taxes) divided by interest and amortization expenses.

[6] Both here and subsequently the term "borrowing cost" refers to the nominal rate. The reader should bear in mind that the relation between the sample companies and their lenders is one of trading present money for future money and that the nominal interest rate is but one facet of the "terms of trade" between them. The compensating balance requirement which the lender imposes upon the company, the pledge of assets required (if any), and the likelihood of renewing the line of credit all act, given any nominal interest rate, to determine the actual cost to the company. Unfortunately, the only interest charge that appears in our data is the nominal rate. Even though the nominal rate to two borrowers may be the same, the actual rate may still differ in one or more of its "invisible dimensions." Even if completely reliable cost estimates were available, they would allow only a statement that the differences observed in the "nominal" rates do, or do not, seem justified by cost differences. It might, in addition, be possible to say something about the probable direction of the "invisible" components of the rates, but these remain essentially unquantifiable.

[7] The breakdown among size categories is arbitrary. (Categorization is based on average asset size for the sample companies during the 1962–64 period.)

CHART 19

Company Size and Cost of Borrowing

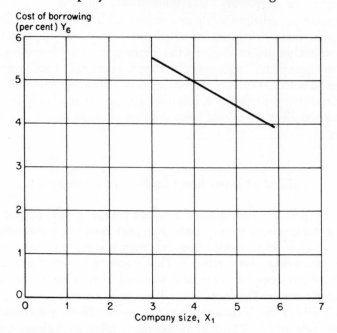

Cost of borrowing
(per cent) Y_6

Company size, X_1

NOTE: The chart is based on the following equation:

$$Y_6 = .0714 - .0048 X_1,$$

where Y_6 is average interest and amortization costs for 1962–64 as a percentage of average negotiated borrowings and X_1 is company size expressed in terms of the log of total assets to the base 10. The simple r is .56 and the adjusted r^2 is .30. The coefficient for X_1 is significant at the .01 level.

by Chart 19. Certain obvious factors help to explain the larger companies' lower borrowings costs. The larger firms have higher burden coverages, as revealed in the table. The higher burden coverages of the larger companies purport greater lender safety and undoubtedly contribute to the lower borrowing rates obtained from lenders by these companies. Also, the broader access of the larger firms to the funds markets places them in a better position to obtain less costly instruments of financing. Yet these explanations for the larger companies' borrowing cost advantage are incomplete. The following paragraphs attempt to establish more precise origins of the larger companies' lower borrowing costs.

TABLE 31

Cost of Borrowing and Burden Coverage in Percentages for Consumer
Finance Sample by Size of Company, 1962–64

Asset Size Group ($ million)	No. of Companies	Cost of Borrowing[a]	Average Burden Coverage
Above $500	2	4.30	3.43
$150–500	6	4.58	2.25
$50–150	4	4.60	2.02
$10–$50	12	5.17	1.92
$5–$10	13	5.21	1.74
$1–$5	11	5.45	1.72
Average for 48 companies		5.08	—

[a] Cost of borrowing equals average debt servicing charges, 1962–64, divided by average amount of negotiated borrowing at year end.

Composition of Liabilities and Cost of Borrowing

Variations in borrowing costs among the sample companies invariably can be traced to differences in the composition of their liabilities. And differences in liability composition are more closely associated with variations in company size than with any other identified factor. Charts 20–22 portray the relation between company size and each of the following liabilities for the sample companies: senior debt as a percentage of total negotiated borrowings, short-term bank loans as a percentage of total negotiated borrowings, and commercial paper outstanding as a percentage of total negotiated borrowings. As indicated in the notes to the charts, the relations between company size and reliance on each of the financing instruments are highly significant.

In Table 32 the various liability proportions are broken down and averaged for the six size classifications. Several facts are evident from inspection of this table. The largest companies place substantially greater reliance on senior long-term debt, as noted earlier; senior long-term debt comprises twice as large a percentage of the total sources of the two largest companies than for the other size categories. The table also suggests the extent to which the smallest classes depend upon short-term borrowing from commercial banks; the percentage of total sources represented by short-term bank loans increases without interruption as size category declines, and is about seven times as great for the smallest classes as for the two largest firms. The percentages in

CHART 20

Company Size and Nonsubordinated Long-Term Debt as Percentage of Total Borrowing

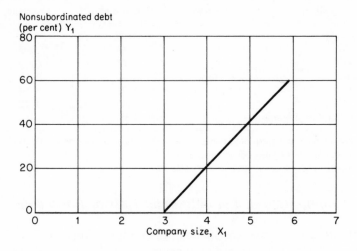

Nonsubordinated debt (per cent) Y_1

Company size, X_1

NOTE: The chart is based on the following equation:

$$Y_1 = -.63 + .20 \, X_1,$$

where Y_1 is nonsubordinated long-term debt as a proportion of total negotiated borrowings and X_1 is company size expressed in terms of the log of total assets to the base 10 ($ thousand). The simple r is .70 and the adjusted r^2 is .48. The regression coefficient for X_1 is significant at the .01 level.

the table suggest that large firms place a comparatively heavy emphasis on commercial paper for their short-term financing needs.

LONG-TERM FINANCING

Table 33 contains percentages of senior and subordinated debt as proportions of total long-term financing for the various size classes. It can be seen from the percentages that reliance upon senior long-term debt increases with size, for companies above $10 million. The largest firms rely on senior long-term debt for 95 per cent of their long-term financing.

The size of the smaller firms and the comparatively modest magnitude of their fund needs preclude public offerings of senior issues.

CHART 21

Company Size and Short-Term Borrowing from Commercial Banks as Proportion of Total Borrowing

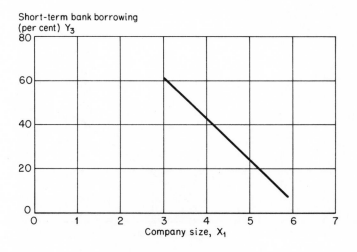

NOTE: The chart is based on the following equation:

$$Y_3 = 1.23 - .19 \, X_1,$$

where Y_3 is short-term commercial bank borrowing as a proportion of total negotiated borrowing and X_1 is company size expressed in terms of the log of total assets to the base 10. The simple r is .59 and the adjusted r^2 is .33. The regression coefficient for X_1 is significant at the .01 level.

Occasionally, companies in the $5–$50-million size range have placed senior long-term issues directly with the life insurance companies and with other institutional investors. Very little reliable information is available concerning the borrowing costs associated with these direct placements, since the terms have generally not been made public. Moreover, actual borrowing costs are extremely hazardous to estimate in any event because of the equity "sweeteners" attached to many of these instruments.[8]

[8] It has been suggested by underwriters who are familiar with the terms of recent private placements of the consumer finance companies that the small firms typically pay higher rates for senior long-term debt than is required for comparable private placements of the larger companies. The higher rates in the senior long-

CHART 22

Company Size and Commercial Paper as Proportion of Total Borrowing

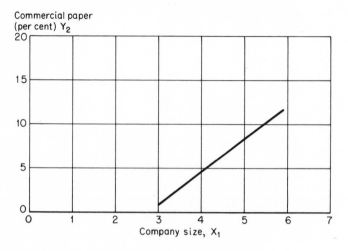

NOTE: The chart is based on the following equation:

$$Y_2 = -.12 + .04 X_1,$$

where Y_2 is commercial paper as a proportion of total negotiated borrowings and X_1 is company size expressed in terms of the log of total assets to the base 10. The simple r is .45 and the adjusted r^2 is .18. The regression coefficient for X_1 is significant at the .01 level.

Table 33 also underscores the smaller companies' comparatively heavy reliance on subordinated debt. This phenomenon may reflect in part the small companies' difficulties in obtaining senior long-term debt. Subordinated debt may be used in place of senior long-term debt to achieve a viable term structure of liabilities. An alternative explanation, however, is that lenders have demanded a larger risk bearing base to support the smaller companies' senior indebtedness. Table 34 reveals that the risk-bearing base for the largest com-

term debt market for offerings of smaller-sized companies probaby represent risk premiums demanded by institutional lenders from these borrowers. They may also reflect the absence of the public market as an alternative source of funds for these companies.

TABLE 32

Liabilities of Sample Consumer Finance Companies by Size of Company, 1962–64
(as percentage of negotiated borrowings)

Asset Size Group ($ million)	No. of Companies	Short Term			Long Term		
		Bank	Commercial Paper	Dealer	Senior Debt	Subordinated	Total
Above $500	2	8.0	5.5	.2	81.8	4.5	100
$150–$500	6	23.9	14.7	9.9	35.4	16.2	100
$50–$150	4	29.3	18.0	4.8	28.3	19.7	100
$10–$50	12	38.1	5.6	1.3	28.0	27.1	100
$5–$10	13	54.4	4.9	3.5	12.2	25.0	100
$1–$5	11	56.8	5.4	5.9	10.9	21.0	100
Average for all sample companies	48	43.0	7.5	4.2	23.0	22.2	100

Note: Percentages may not add to 100 due to rounding.

TABLE 33

Senior and Subordinated Debt as Percentages of Total Long-Term Debt
by Size of Company, 1962–64

Size of Company	Senior Long-Term Debt	Subordinated Junior and Senior Debt
	Total Debt	Total Long-Term Debt
Above $500 million	95	5
$150–$500 million	69	31
$50–$150 million	54	46
$10–$50 million	51	49
$5–$10 million	32	68
$1–$5 million	34	66

panies supported 2.18 times of senior borrowing in comparison with 1.60 times or less for the three smallest loan company groups. Many smaller firms apparently have preferred to issue subordinated debt despite its comparatively high cost rather than contribute more equity capital. Regardless of the precise rationale, companies with less than $50 million in assets have relied to a substantially larger degree on subordinated debt, which has been more costly than senior debt instruments, and hence the higher cost of long-term indebtedness for the smaller firm.

TABLE 34

Borrowing Ratios and Proportions for Consumer Finance Sample
by Size of Company, 1962–64

Asset Size Group ($ million)	No. of Companies	Total Senior Borrowing Risk-Bearing Base[b]	Total Senior Borrowing as Percentage of Total Assets[c]	Total Borrowing[a] as Percentage of Total Assets[c]
Above 500	2	2.18	64.6	67.5
150–500	6	2.11	64.9	77.4
50–150	4	1.76	61.5	76.5
10–50	12	1.36	56.0	67.5
5–10	13	1.38	57.3	76.6
1–5	11	1.60	60.8	76.5
Average for all sample companies	48	1.56	59.4	76.5

[a] Total borrowing = All negotiated claims, i.e., senior debt plus subordinated debt.

[b] Risk-bearing base = Equity plus junior and senior subordinated debt.

[c] Total assets is defined to exclude unearned income.

SHORT-TERM FINANCING

A combination of cost and risk considerations points to bank borrowing or to the maintenance of bank lines as the keystone of short-term financing by virtually all consumer finance companies irrespective of size. However, differentials between bank loan and commercial paper rates appear to influence the composition of short-term borrowing by companies whose asset size exceeds $50 million. Money-market skills together with favorable internal costs have made it possible in the past for some firms to take advantage of favorable rates in the commercial paper market.[9] In Table 35, which depicts commerical paper issuances as a percentage of total short-term financing for the six size classes, the greater reliance on commercial paper for short-term needs by the larger companies can readily be seen; commercial paper as a percentage of short-term negotiated borrowings increases dramatically with increases in size class. Smaller companies are largely confined to bank borrowing to satisfy their short-term needs. Most companies in the $1- to $50-million size range

[9] For a definitive examination of conditions of entry and levels of activity in the commercial paper market between 1920 and 1961, see Richard T. Selden, *Trends and Cycles in the Commercial Paper Market, New York,* 1963.

TABLE 35
Commercial Paper Issuance as Percentage of Short-Term Financing
by Size of Company, 1962–64

Asset Size Group ($ million)	Commercial Paper as Percentage of Total Short-Term Financing
Above $500 million	67
$150–$500 million	66
$50–$150 million	53
$10–$50 million	14
$5–$10 million	7
$1–$5 million	8

are formally excluded from the commercial paper market because of their size.

Most smaller companies are confined to bank borrowing to satisfy their short-term needs. In order to issue commercial paper, dealers require that the size of a company's net worth plus subordinated indebtedness serve as a base for commercial paper flotations. Most companies in the $1–$50 million size range are formally excluded from the commercial paper markets on the basis of this criterion and consequently are deprived of the associated advantages of low-cost open-market rates.

The chief and virtually the only options in external short-term financing of the consumer finance companies are bank loans and the issuance of commercial paper. (Outside these channels only thrift certificates and certificates of deposit are generally available, and these instruments are of relatively minor importance.) Chart 23 is a history of the prime bank rate and the commercial paper rate offered by the largest dealer in recent years. It is clear from the chart that during the 1962–64 period the commercial paper rate has almost always been lower than the bank rate, and that this rate differential has contributed to significantly lower borrowing costs for the large companies that are the principal issuers of commercial paper.[10] Since 1965, tight credit conditions have contributed to higher open-market rates than bank rates, and this phenomenon has persisted throughout 1966. Thus, the relative advantage in lower borrowing costs of commercial paper which the larger companies previously enjoyed has vanished during the recent tight-money period. The larger companies

[10] The actual open market-bank rate cost differential is difficult to measure. It reflects not only differences in nominal rates but also differences in compensating balance requirements and other requirements which change from time to time.

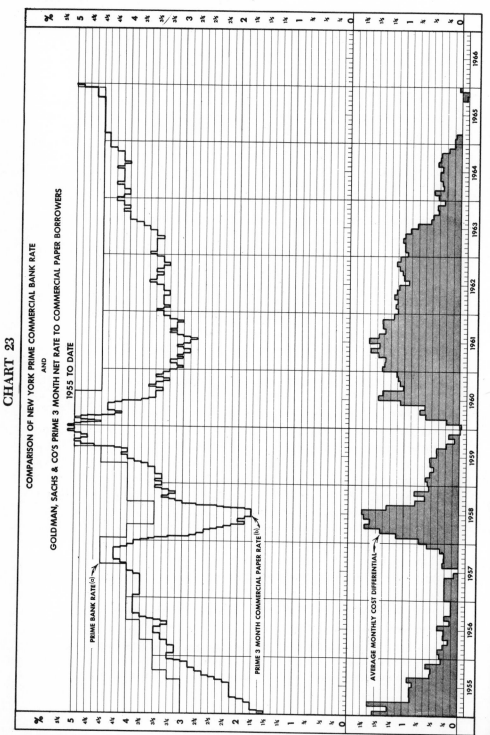

CHART 23

COMPARISON OF NEW YORK PRIME COMMERCIAL BANK RATE
AND
GOLDMAN, SACHS & CO'S PRIME 3 MONTH NET RATE TO COMMERCIAL PAPER BORROWERS

1955 TO DATE

PRIME BANK RATE (a)

PRIME 3 MONTH COMMERCIAL PAPER RATE (b)

AVERAGE MONTHLY COST DIFFERENTIAL

NOTE TO CHART 23

NOTE: The prime bank rate is the nominal rate quoted on a discount basis. The commercial paper rate shown is also a discount rate. The rate includes the dealer's commissions for marketing the paper. The chart does not include the imputed costs of compensating bank balances maintained either by bank borrowers or commercial paper issuers. (Both bank borrowers and commercial paper issuers are required to maintain compensating bank balances. Compensating balances support bank borrowers' lines of credit. Unused lines of credit must be maintained by commercial paper issuers to support commercial paper borrowings; these credit lines provide the commercial paper issuers with an alternative source of financing in the event that commercial paper buyers become scarce.)

ᵃ Disregarding cost of compensating balances.

ᵇ Total cost to borrowers including all charges.

have continued to tap the commercial paper market since 1965 notwithstanding the recent unfavorable rate differential due to the shortage of available bank credit.

Degree of Leverage and Borrowing Costs

Table 34 arrays borrowing ratios for the different size categories. Both the ratio of senior borrowing to risk-bearing base and senior borrowing as a percentage of total assets reveal a positive association between size of company and senior borrowing. Equally significant, however, is the lack of apparent correlation between size class and *total* borrowing as a percentage of total assets. Total borrowing as a percentage of total assets is virtually identical for each size class except for the largest and one medium-size category, whose total debt percentages are conspicuously lower. In effect, the smaller size classes appear to have maintained their total debt percentages by employing comparatively large proportions of bank loans and subordinated debt. And the subordinated debt is more costly than senior debt, thus contributing to relatively high borrowing costs for the smaller companies.

The principal device for limiting risk exposure of the consumer finance companies' creditors is quantitative limitations of senior debt incurred relative to the risk-bearing base. It should be emphasized, however, that although the smaller companies' lower proportions of senior debt to total assets imply more restrictive lending limits, a number of other factors also influence the borrowing proportions. Many firms undoubtedly have not borrowed maximum allowable amounts, and consequently their balance-sheet proportions do not reflect borrowing limits. Moreover, end-of-fiscal-year balance sheets may in some instances represent a seasonal low in assets and borrowings. In these instances, the ratio between senior claims and the risk-bearing base will be at its low. With these qualifications, however, the senior borrowing to risk-bearing base ratios in Table 34 seem to reveal that lenders grant substantially more liberal borrowing limits to larger companies, particularly those in the two largest size classes.[11]

Term Structure of Liabilities and Borrowing Costs

Given that debt has been elected in preference to equity by a consumer finance company, the choice between short-term and long-term debt may partially reflect the company's judgment on short versus long interest rates. Alternative judgments yield different returns because there can be differences in short- and long-term interest rates at a moment in time, and because these differences fluctuate through time. In the endeavor to minimize interest costs, a company can substitute short- for long-term debt and vice versa, since shifts in the term structure of interest rates alter the relative costs of short- and long-term commitments in the futures markets for money.

Although there is no way to infer directly management's objectives in the short-long-term selection, it is assumed that the primary consideration has been the establishment of a maturity schedule of liabilities which is consistent with cash flows to be yielded by the asset structures.[12] By tailoring its debt maturities to coincide with or to lag asset realization, a company can avoid the pressures of short-term

[11] The senior debt ratios for sales finance companies, including captive finance companies, are somewhat higher than those of consumer finance companies, running to five and six times the borrowing base in some instances. Lenders agree that the sales finance companies deserve the higher ratios because of the comparatively high quality of their receivables. Presumably the investments of these companies are better risks. Yet many sales finance companies are characterized by substantial portfolio concentration in comparatively high-risk wholesale paper. The usual concentration of captive sales finance companies' receivables within a single industry and the resulting lack of diversification may well result in risk levels as high as (or higher than) those characteristic of consumer finance companies. It is not surprising that consumer finance industry spokesman have argued that consumer finance companies should be allowed borrowing ratios similar to those offered the sales finance companies and the captive borrowers.

[12] The attempt to establish a viable maturity schedule of liabilities may dictate a capital structure which does not minimize interest costs.

liabilities on cash flows.[13] Disregard of this financial dictate renders the offending company vulnerable to a sudden contraction of available short-term funds.

Over the years there has been a secular trend toward consumer loans with longer maturities. As a consequence the collection period for consumer finance company receivables has lengthened and cash flow considerations have warranted extending debt maturities. Chart 24, which is based on a simple correlation between company size and long-term financing as a percentage of total negotiated borrowings, reveals that larger companies rely more heavily on long-term financing than smaller firms. This tendency is also evident in Table 32, where long-term and short-term percentages are calculated for the different size categories.

By using long-term debt instruments more extensively, the larger firms have probably been able to maintain a more viable liquidity position. It has been possible for them to float long-term senior debt issues confidently in view of the predictable, sustained growth in demand for consumer credit; for the most part, it has been unnecessary to rely on the flexibility afforded by short-term debt in adjusting to contractions in receivables, since prolonged contractions have appeared unlikely.

At the same time (and most important for our purposes), the comparatively heavy reliance on long-term debt during recent years due to liquidity considerations has proved to be a good term-structure judgment. As interest rates have risen, the comparatively heavy emphasis on long-term instruments has yielded lower interest costs than would otherwise have been possible. Thus, the relatively long-term structures of the larger companies' liabilities have afforded not only liquidity benefits but also cost advantages.

Conclusion

We have suggested that company size is the most important determinant of differences among the sample companies in borrowing costs. The lower costs can be traced both to differences in debt composition and to the larger companies' comparatively long-term structures of

---

[13] The "ideal formula," according to Howard and Upton, a rule venerated by many practitioners, is that "short-term assets should be financed short-term and long-term should be financed long-term." Howard and Upton, *Introduction to Business Finance*, pp. 310–314.

CHART 24

Company Size and Long-Term Debt as Percentage of Total Negotiated Borrowings

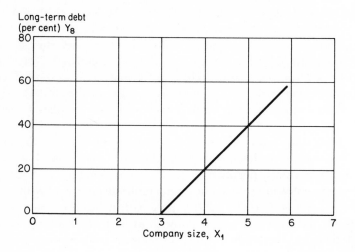

NOTE: The chart is based on the following equation:

$$Y_8 = -.6257 + .1997 \, X_1,$$

where Y_8 is long-term debt as a proportion of total negotiated debt and X_1 is company size expressed in terms of the log of total assets to the base 10. The simple r is .70 and the adjustedt r^2 is .48. The regression coefficient for X_1 is significant at the .01 level.

debt obligations. The larger companies rely heavily on senior long-term issues and place greater emphasis than small firms on commercial paper for short-term financing needs. By way of contrast, the smaller firms are largely restricted to commercial banks for their external financing needs. Finally, the facts strongly suggest that creditors have imposed more restrictive debt limits on the smaller firms, albeit the evidence on this point is inconclusive.

VI

Conclusions for Regulation

ROBERT W. JOHNSON

Krannert Graduate School of Industrial Administration,
Purdue University

On the fiftieth anniversary of the First Draft of the Uniform Small
Loan Law, it seems appropriate to re-examine the concepts and principles expressed in that law. As explained in Chapter I, it was originally formulated as an antidote to rapacious illegal lenders by providing
an exception to existing usury laws so that legal lenders could provide
credit at reasonable rates. To a large extent the small-loan companies
that entered the market at that time held semimonopolistic positions.
There were few alternatives, only scattered credit unions, remedial
loan associations, and a few Morris Plan Banks. The economy was
becoming industrialized; the farm population still exceeded the urban;
and relatively few people possessed an advanced education. Against
this background it is not surprising that the First Draft provided for
rigorous and detailed regulation so that legal lenders could provide
credit to consumers at reasonable rates.

While times have changed, much of the basic philosophy of the
First Draft of the Uniform Small Loan Law was continued through
seven drafts, ending in 1942. The last draft still provides the legal
framework for the operations of consumer finance companies under
small-loan laws, even though they now face vigorous direct and indirect competition from credit unions, sales finance companies, retailers, and commercial banks. The concentration of population in

137

urban centers has provided consumers with many alternate sources of sales and cash credit, and the higher level of consumer education, while not perfect, has encouraged consumers to shop more widely for credit. In short, whereas at one time most consumers needed the protection of small-loan legislation, now only a portion of those who use consumer credit benefit from the strict laws governing consumer finance companies. Under these circumstances the laws need re-evaluation.

Re-evaluation of the legal environment for cash loans to consumers is particularly appropriate at this time in view of the project undertaken by the National Conference of Commissioners on Uniform State Laws to draft uniform consumer credit legislation. While that proposal covers the entire consumer credit industry, many of the principles set forth here may be applicable to other segments of the industry.

Development of recommendations for regulation is complicated by the existence of varying legal environments for cash loans among the states. Some states have only a law patterned after the Uniform Small Loan Law, but with widely differing ceilings on rates and sizes of loans. Numerous other less significant adjustments to the Uniform Small Loan Law have been made by various states. A number have enacted ancillary acts permitting larger loans than allowed by the existing Small Loan Law. While this varied legal environment makes interpretation of data very difficult, it also means that recommendations for regulation need to be couched in very general terms. Proposals suitable for a state with only a Small Loan Law may not be equally applicable to a state that also has an ancillary act.

To avoid this problem to some extent, the discussion that follows relates most directly to possible regulations that might be incorporated in a Uniform Consumer Credit Code. This Code would replace existing Small Loan laws and ancillary acts and other state laws regulating cash lenders. This is a useful form of presentation, since it can then be assumed that all cash lenders would be subject to essentially the same rules of disclosure of finance charges as time rates and dollars amounts and the same set of restrictions on debtors' and creditors' remedies. However, the discussion will also suggest the direction that amendments to existing laws might take if a uniform code is not enacted.

The analysis of the data in the preceding chapters provides insights into three main areas of regulation of consumer finance companies: ceilings on consumer finance charges, ceilings on size of loan, and limitations upon the number of offices. While this list by no means exhausts the entire body of regulations surrounding consumer finance companies, these are the areas in which this study provides significant light. It should be emphasized that areas not covered by this study deserve research as well. Special consideration needs to be directed to such areas as personal bankruptcies, deficiency judgments, garnishments, wage assignments, the holder-in-due-course concept, administrative controls, and various forms of credit and property insurance. That these topics were not covered in this study is not due to their lack of importance, but because the various authors have a limited life span. Nothing said here should be taken as a suggestion that responsible protection for borrowers of small amounts should be curtailed.

Ceilings on Consumer Finance Charges

As shown in Chapter I, consumer finance companies provide a distinctive service in the cash credit market. As compared with other cash lenders, consumer finance companies generally make small loans to riskier borrowers. As risk managers, the personnel of consumer finance companies must screen applicants with special care and provide counseling and adjustments to loan contracts. Since risk management is a personal service, wages and salaries make up almost half of the total operating expenses of the sample of companies studied in Chapter II. Coupled with the relatively small size of credit extensions, these costs explain in large part the comparatively high operating cost per $100 of average outstanding credit at consumer finance companies.

WHY ANY CEILING ON RATES?

Since these costs must be covered if the service is to be performed, it is natural to inquire why there should be a ceiling on the finance charges of consumer finance companies. Ours is an economy that is relatively free from price controls; indeed, the free price system is basic to our economic system. While the prices charged by public utilities are subject to control, the discussion of Chapter I demonstrates that consumer finance companies are subject to competition, especially with respect to larger loans. All credit grantors compete vigorously for consumers with good credit standings, and the advent of higher ceilings and ancillary loan acts has brought consumer finance companies into sharper competition with commercial banks, sales finance companies, and other credit grantors.

In addition there is usually vigorous competition among consumer finance companies for consumers whose credit standing may be unacceptable to other cash lenders, since rates permitted these lenders are too low to allow them to serve this market profitably.

The public demand for control of the price of credit probably stems from ancient beliefs about the sterility of money and the apparent injustice of charging for a service not provided by human labor. Even this philosophy, however irrational, does not apply to the major part of the charges for the services of consumer finance companies. Only about one-third of the income received by consumer finance companies in 1960–64 can be taken as representing "forbearance," that is, the charge for a delay in collecting a debt.[1] The balance is composed of various operating expenses required by the services involved in risk management.

Thus, while rigid regulation of finance charges on all cash loans to consumers may have been justified in 1916, the need for such price control has diminished as more cash lenders have entered the field and as larger loans have been permitted. Currently, price controls are still needed on loans where lenders are allowed a higher rate than might be permitted as a general ceiling on cash loans. The form of a possible rate structure is illustrated in the diagram:

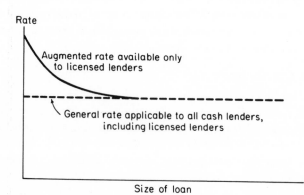

Rate

Augmented rate available only to licensed lenders

General rate applicable to all cash lenders, including licensed lenders

Size of loan

Limitations upon the augmented rate are necessary because loans of this size and type are most likely to involve consumers who

[1] Average operating expenses of $13.17 were about double pretax costs of equity and nonequity funds in 1960–64 (Table 5, Chapter II).

find licensed lenders as credit sources of last resort. Without any limit on rates, some companies might take advantage of such consumers by charging unconscionable rates. Credit grantors electing to charge the augmented rates probably must accept a larger measure of supervision and control than those restricting their charges to the lower, general rate.

While a ceiling on augmented finance charges appears to be economically and socially justified, the wider competition among those offering large dollar amounts of both vendor and lender credit makes it more difficult to support a general price ceiling on all cash credit to consumers. In this connection it is explicitly assumed that a Uniform Consumer Credit Code would have some form of time-rate disclosure. This type of disclosure, in addition to careful shopping for credit by consumers, should often force rates below the general ceiling, especially for larger loans. Of course, there will still be some ignorant and overeager consumers and avaricious credit grantors when large loans are involved. In all fields other than credit, society generally applies the rule of *caveat emptor*. If a consumer pays $2,000 more than he should for a house or lot, there is no mechanism of price control to remedy his ignorance, carelessness, or greed.

However, in the field of credit it would be naïve not to recognize that the long history of sentiments relating to usury makes it politically inexpedient at this time to remove a general rate ceiling on consumer credit transactions, even those above a certain dollar amount. To deal with this problem, we have two alternatives: (1) abolish general ceilings, but permit a court test of unconscionable contracts, as is the case in England, or (2) establish relatively high general ceilings in an attempt to rule out the more extreme finance rates. In view of the uncertainty to the industry and costs to the consumer of testing contracts before courts, it seems preferable to accept the second alternative. Thus, the general ceiling should exceed the normal, competitive market rate on large loans, but be below the augmented rates permitted on smaller loans by licensed lenders.

We are left, then, with the task of designing ceilings that will nip unconscionable transactions, but still allow the industry to operate with the economic freedom accorded most other concerns serving the American consumer. As the size of credit involved increases, the rationale for the ceilings rests less on economic and social reasons and more on emotional and political biases.

TABLE 36

Net Profits After Taxes to Equity Funds of Nine Major Consumer Finance
Companies, Manufacturing Corporations, and Commercial Banks,
1960–64
(per cent)

Year	Nine Major Consumer Finance Companies[a]	Private Manufacturing Corporations[b]	Insured Commercial Banks[c]
1960	11.4	9.1	10.0
1961	11.8	8.7	9.4
1962	11.8	9.6	8.8
1963	12.3	10.1	8.9
1964	12.2	11.4	8.7

[a] Table 16, Chapter II.

[b] Data on a comparable basis are not available prior to 1958. *Economic Report of the President*, January 1966, Washington, 1966, p. 285.

[c] Ratio of net income to total capital accounts of all insured commercial banks. *Federal Reserve Bulletin*, July, 1962, p. 903; July, 1966, p. 1046.

THE LEVEL OF RATE CEILINGS

A ceiling on prices is almost certain to produce a different allocation of resources than if the setting of prices were left to the forces of the market. Interference with the market will affect the level of service afforded consumers and is also very likely to change the structure of the industry. While these effects will be discussed in order, it is worth noting that a change in the structure of the industry will, in turn, influence the nature and cost of services provided consumers.

Effect on Consumers. The ratios of net profits to equity funds of the nine major consumer finance companies are compared to similar ratios of industrial corporations and commercial banks in Table 36 for the period 1960–64. The data are not wholly comparable, since the sample of manufacturing corporations is much broader than for the consumer finance companies. As observed with reference to Table 28, Chapter IV, the "four large companies had . . . higher net operating income ratios than did other licensed lenders in the thirty states." Thus the bias introduced by the small sample of the nine major companies overstates the profit ratios of the industry. As might be expected, commercial banks, with their higher quality loans of all types and fairly rigid restrictions on entry to protect depositors, generally `showed the lowest return on equity of the three groups represented. While the evidence is not conclusive, it suggests that the major consumer finance companies do not make profits that are significantly out of line with those earned in other types of business when differences in risk are considered.[2]

This type of analysis implies that the ceilings on consumer finance charges should be established so that they are high enough to cover costs and provide a "reasonable" profit to lenders.[3] However, this approach puts the cart before the horse. To a profit-seeking enterprise, ceilings on rates determine the allowable level of costs which, in turn, are a product of the level of service provided. More directly, other things being equal, ceilings on rates determine which consumers can be served by legitimate credit grantors and which must forgo use of credit or turn to illegal lenders. If ceilings were lowered, consumers who were only marginally creditworthy and costly to serve would be driven from the legal market. If ceilings were raised, less creditworthy consumers would be accepted by credit grantors whose operating costs would then rise to reflect their more extensive collection efforts and higher bad-debt losses. In short, companies adjust their costs to the rate ceilings in order to produce the level of profits required by the freely competitive capital markets for this type of business. Thus, whether rates are high or low, we would not expect to find profits "out of line" once the industry has adjusted to the schedule of rates. What will be out of line if rates are too low is the level of service provided consumers by legal lenders.

There is considerable evidence in the preceding chapters to support the hypothesis that costs follow rate ceilings, rather than

[2] Based on rankings of the return on total capital (common stock, preferred stock, long-term debt, and minority interests), an earlier study placed the consumer finance industry 29th out of 33 major industrial groups, 1953–57. The difference between these results and those presented in Table 36 are attributable in large part to the inclusion of long-term debt in the base. Sidney Cottle, "The Earnings Performance of the Consumer Finance Industry," *Journal of Finance,* September 1960, pp. 387–406.

[3] The Small Loans Regulatory Board of Massachusetts explicitly follows this approach: "In regard to the licensed lenders engaged in the business to be regulated, we find that a fair and reasonable rate of return upon the assets is 7.4%." Rate Order of April 1, 1960, p. 4. Note that when the financial leverage is favorable, the return on assets will be less than the return on equity funds. "Financial leverage" means the use of funds for which a fixed maximum annual charge is paid (normally, bonds and preferred stock). To obtain favorable financial leverage, the funds obtained must be employed at a higher rate than is paid for their use.

that costs determine these ceilings. For example, the study of the nine largest consumer finance companies shows that "the two companies with the highest charge . . . also had the highest operating costs so that the higher costs offset the earning potential of the higher charges" (Chapter II). Analysis of the broader sample of forty-eight companies reveals that "when gross income per $100 of loans outstanding is high, operating costs per $100 of loans is high and vice versa (Chapter III).[4]

The close association of the rates of gross operating income and operating expenses is explained in large part by differences in risk management. By allowing higher rate ceilings, legislation encourages the acceptance of higher risks among consumers. Persuasive evidence is found in Chapter IV that "higher average rates of gross income do accompany higher average assumption of risk without any apparent incentive in the observed measure of profit" (Table 23). Similarly, Chart 13 in Chapter III shows that net charge-offs are higher on the average as the gross income per $100 of loans outstanding is higher. But the assumption of higher risks not only results in higher bad debts but also "requires higher operating expenses other than that portion involved in provision for loss" (Chapter IV). Thus costs tend to follow ceilings on rates because companies operating in states with high rate ceilings manage more risky portfolios of consumer loans.[5]

Unfortunately, these conclusions make the task of setting rate ceilings more complex. To judge the adequacy of the over-all level of the ceiling, we must look, not at costs or profits, but at the size of the market that is served. We need to know more about who is forced out of the legal market and who is permitted in the market. A measure of the scope of the legal market may be obtained by determining the number and amount of loans outstanding in relation to the population, as in Chapter IV. Where these measures of loan service are low, there may be an inadequate supply of legal credit for consumers. It is obviously difficult to assay the extent of

[4] Recall that the simple r between the gross income ratios and the operating cost ratios was 0.91. Since a "perfect" correlation would be 1.00, the correlation is clearly very strong.

[5] For additional analysis and support of this point, see Maurice B. Goudzwaard, "The Effect of Rate Structure upon the Availability of Credit at Consumer Finance Companies," unpublished Ph.D. dissertation, Michigan State University, 1965.

the illegal market, but a state that finds widespread operations of goon squads and "juice" men might suspect that its ceilings on small-loan rates are too low. Thus rates that are too low do not protect consumers. Instead, they create a large enough market of unsatisfied consumers that illegal lenders find it economical to assume the risks inherent in serving this market. Needless to say, these risks are passed on to consumers in the form of extremely high rates of charge and harsh collection tactics. That consumer finance companies find it necessary to reject about half of all new applicants shows that a significant group of consumers cannot be served under present rate ceilings. The rejection rate also demonstrates the relatively higher costs of serving new, rather than present, borrowers.

In summary, it is not possible to say that a certain ceiling on lending rates is too high or too low. It depends upon the proportion of consumers that one wishes to be served by the legal market. Some who are refused service in the legal market will postpone their use of credit, and this result may be socially desirable. In other instances, however, the need may not be postponable, and consumers will turn to the illegal market served by unlicensed and unregulated lenders. Evidence concerning increasing losses from bad debts and declining profit margins (Chapter II) suggests that if existing legal structures are maintained, consumer finance companies will necessarily become more selective in granting cash loans.

Effect on Industry Structure. Not only does the level of the rate ceiling determine which consumers will be in the market, but which consumer finance companies. Lower rate ceilings force both marginal consumers and marginal companies from the market. It might be noted that this is a rather different effect than in the case of instalment *sales credit.* In the case of vendor credit very low ceilings on finance charges can be offset by a redistribution of the total time price of goods or services between the cash price and the finance charge. Thus if instalment charges were limited to an annual rate, say of 12 per cent, we could anticipate an increase in cash prices and a decrease in finance charges, but quite probably little change in total time prices.

Such adjustments to ceilings on finance charges are not available to cash lenders. Since the granting of credit is not accompanied by the sale of merchandise, cash lenders have no place to bury their finance charges. This is not strictly true in those states that have not adequately regulated premiums for credit insurance.[6] If lower rate ceilings narrow the market for their service, there will be fewer loan services available from fewer consumer finance companies.[7]

How would industry structure be changed if ceilings on consumer finance charges were lowered? The evidence provided indicates that the industry would be more heavily concentrated in the hands of the large lenders. It was observed from Table 28 in Chapter IV that, in comparison to their smaller competitors, "the four large companies had larger average loans outstanding, lower gross income and operating expense ratios, and higher net operating income ratios. . . ." In part these efficiencies may be traceable to their typically higher average number of loans per office (Chapters II and IV). On top of these operating efficiencies, the large companies have a notably lower cost of financing (Chart 19, Chapter V). This is a product of the lower rates at which they borrow, as well as the higher ratios of debt to equity that they can employ.[8] Thus the marginal consumer finance company is probably small on the average, and it would typically be the small company that would be forced from the market if rate ceilings were lowered.

Whether or not it would be desirable to see a greater portion of

[6] Under the pressures of rising costs and fixed ceilings, consumer finance companies have attempted to cushion the squeeze by profiting from the sale of various forms of credit insurance. The increased dependence upon other income of this sort has been noted in Chapter II. However, this is only a temporary expedient, and profits from this source are already being pared. To some extent, this may be attributed to the introduction in a number of states of the model bill regulating credit life insurance prepared by the National Association of Insurance Commissioners.

[7] This has happened; see Rolf Nugent, "Three Experiments with Small-Loan Interest Rates," *Harvard Business Review*, October 1933, pp. 35–46. In three states, at different times the legislatures reduced the rate ceilings in response to public allegations that they were too high and that licensed lenders were making too much profit. Since legitimate lenders could not operate under the reduced rate, they withdrew from the state. To fill the need for consumer loans that still existed, loan sharks flocked back and employed their usual high-handed methods, high rates, and harsh collection tactics. When new legislation providing higher rates was introduced, legitimate lenders returned, and illegal lenders were substantially eliminated.

[8] However, the net advantage to the common stockholders of the higher ratios of debt to equity may not be as great as it might seem. Higher ratios of debt entail larger risks to the residual owners, as well as greater variablility of earnings per share. To the extent that the stock market adjusts for these effects through a lower price-earning ratio, common stockholders may not receive the full benefit implied by a high debt-to-net-worth ratio.

the consumer finance industry concentrated in the hands of the large lenders is a matter of judgment. To the extent that consumer finance companies are lenders of last resort, it would place this degree of monopoly power in the hands of a smaller number of companies. Since large companies emphasize large loans (Chapter IV), it would reduce the services available to the borrower of small amounts. While there may still be some economies of scale that would benefit consumers, the present size of the large companies suggests that most such economies have already been achieved and that significant further economies may not be forthcoming by greater concentration of the industry with the largest firms. While the growing cost-price squeeze will probably continue to force a reduction in the significance of very small companies, there does not appear to be a strong economic argument for hastening the process by lowering ceilings on consumer finance charges.

THE SLOPE OF RATE CEILINGS

Thus far it has been argued that augmented rate ceilings on small loans are more meaningful than general ceilings on all loans. While the general ceilings on rates would be below the augmented rate ceiling, competition would tend to force rates even below the general ceiling, especially on large loans. On small loans competition may force rates below the augmented ceiling, but, even so, more careful attention to the design of this ceiling appears both economically and politically desirable because of the vulnerability of these borrowers.

Augmented rate ceilings on small loans need to bear some relationship to costs of operation. This is not because of a desire to charge a rate that is "fair" to each individual consumer. This is an impossible goal. The charge for a one-year loan of $500 that is just barely adequate for a marginal consumer with very poor credit standing is relatively "unfair" to a consumer with better credit standing. In order to obtain a "fair" rate, each consumer must shop around to find the rate appropriate to his credit standing and the type of credit service desired. Thus rate ceilings on small loans must be related to costs, not in order to be "fair" to consumers, but so that the structure of the ceiling does not distort the supply of loans of certain sizes or maturities within the total market. This point was well illustrated in Chapter IV, where it was shown that Maryland's level rate ceiling greatly discourages the making of very small loans, whereas the steeply sloped rate ceiling in Alabama produces a significantly higher percentage of loans under $100.

Costs of operation are clearly related to the size and maturity of loan. Thus formulating ceilings on consumer finance charges in relation to costs of operation becomes a multidimensional problem. In theory, the ceiling should be related to both the amount of the loan and its maturity. However, since long maturities are characteristically associated with large loans, it has been the practice in most states to relate the rate ceilings to size of loan.

To relate the ceiling to the size of loan, it should be recalled that a substantial portion of the costs that accompany personal risk management is fixed, regardless of the amount of the loan. Examination of Tables 5 and 8 in Chapter II shows that the relatively fixed costs of salary, occupancy, and advertising make up a large portion of total operating expenses. While cost of capital invested in outstanding loans varies directly with the amount of each loan, there is some evidence that the risk of bad debts may be less than proportional to the amount borrowed.

The large element of fixed costs has been recognized in most state laws fixing rate ceilings on loans by licensed lenders. Typically, rate ceilings decline as the size of loan increases. The problem at hand is whether the rate of decline, or slope, of the rate ceiling is appropriate. Evidence from this study sheds some light on the problem. In Chapter III it was found that operating costs as a percentage of loans outstanding among forty-eight companies decline an average of $1.26 for each $100 increase in average loan size, if the other variables studied are held constant at their means. The same tendency for costs to decline as loan size increases is found in Table 22 of Chapter IV. Here expense ratios per $100 of average loan balance outstanding range from 32.8 per cent for an average balance of $131 to 16.2 per cent at $400 and 11.0 per cent at $588.

It was observed in Chapter II that the average loan size has increased substantially over the past several years. If this trend continues so that loan sizes are beyond the range of observed values in this study, the line depicting the average relation between loan size and operating costs (Chart 8, Chapter III) will obviously not continue as a straight line for larger sizes of loan. (If so, we would eventually have zero operating costs per $100 of loans outstanding— a truly remarkable level of efficiency.) Instead, as the industry moves to larger and larger loans, the ratio of operating costs to average size of loan will decline at a diminishing rate.

The bearing of the cost structure presented in Chapter III upon the ceilings on small loans is subject to two additional qualifications. In the first place, these are average costs per dollar of outstanding amounts of loans and may not directly enter a lender's decision as to whether or not to grant credit to a particular loan applicant. Second, the average loan size represents a mixture of large and small loans for companies operating in many different states, with corresponding variations in economic and demographic characteristics and regulations governing licensed lenders.

It is possible to remove the influence of interstate variations in operating conditions and consider the behavior of direct unit costs per loan account by reviewing findings from a study prepared by Comiskey in 1965.[9] His findings relate the direct operating costs in some 400 branch loan offices located within a state to the average loan size in each branch office. Data were separately tabulated for four different states (Table 37).

TABLE 37
Increase in Unit Cost per $100 Increase in Average Loan Size

State	Unit Cost Increase[a]
A	$2.46
B	2.44
C	1.51
D	.58

[a] The data express the relation between direct operating costs and average loan size while holding the average number of accounts, delinquency rate, wage level index, proportion of total loans made to new borrowers, and acceptance rate of new loan applications constant at their average. Direct branch operating costs include all locally incurred and paid expense items. They do not include interest costs, taxes, bad debts, and certain expenses, chiefly home office administration, that were allocated to the branches. Source: Comiskey, "Loan Cost Behavior," p. 106.

These data represent differences in direct costs among branch offices in given states and not variations *within* a branch office due to differences in size of loan. Thus the differences in direct lending costs serve as a partial or indirect measure of marginal direct lending costs, but not a direct measure.

The data are informative in several respects. First, the very significant difference in the behavior of direct lending costs among the four states demonstrates that companies operating in different groups of states are substantially affected by the wide variations in state small-loan laws and regulations, as well as by economic and demographic

[9] Eugene E. Comiskey, "A Study of Loan Cost Behavior in Consumer Finance Companies," unpublished Ph.D. dissertation, Michigan State University, 1965.

differences. Second, direct costs are not fixed, regardless of size of loan. Large loans entail additional expenditures, possibly in the form of investigating the applicant and effecting a security interest in collateral.

Finally, the data from the Comiskey study suggest that direct costs do not rise as rapidly in relation to size of loan as the finance charges permitted by existing ceilings. In these four industrial states,[10] permitted finance charges on twelve-month loans averaged $18.71 on $100 balances and $51.42 on $300 balances. Thus the difference of $200 in initial loan balance could be accompanied by a variation of $32.71 in the finance charge. Part of the difference may be accounted for by the added cost of capital invested in the larger loan and a reward for the assumption of risk. If we assume this to be 10 per cent of the additional average balance, we can explain $10 of the $32.71 added charge. (Note that the average added balance is about $100, not $200, because of the declining monthly unpaid balance.) This leaves $22.71 to be accounted for on the basis of incremental direct costs. As may be seen from Table 37, the growth in direct lending costs per $100 increase in average loan size ranges from $0.58 to $2.46. These differences fall far short of explaining the net differential of $22.71.[11]

Thus the analysis indicates that the borrower of $300 may be getting a "bargain," but that the borrower of $100 is obtaining an even greater "bargain." If there is absolute discrimination, it must exist on much larger loans, possibly those above $1,000. This conclusion is supported in part by the analysis of earnings (before interest and taxes) and average loan size in Chapter III (Chart 13).

Does this analysis suggest that existing rate ceilings should be more steeply sloped to reduce the apparent discrimination in favor of those who borrow very small amounts? From an economic point of view the discrimination is probably not as great as it might seem. Many a small loan is made (both by consumer finance companies and by other types of lenders) to establish a position as a credit grantor to a customer whose needs currently are small, but who at a later date may have larger, more profit-yielding needs. Credit grantors can also count on relatively lower servicing costs on renewals than on new applications. Thus the pertinent gross income is not that derived from a single transaction, but from the total experience that may eventually develop between the credit grantor and his customer.

[10] The four large industrial states selected are not revealed in the study.

[11] Comiskey also finds that risk is lower for larger loans, *ibid.*, pp. 111–117. The general analysis of relative discrimination among loans by size is based on pp. 147–149 of his dissertation.

Even allowing for the point noted above, some relative discrimination probably exists, although it is difficult to quantify. Justification for this discrimination falls more in the realm of public policy than economics. If very small loans were required to carry their "fair share" of costs, the consequent rate might be regarded as exorbitant. Nonetheless, discrimination which favors borrowers of small loans may ultimately pinch off lending in small amounts, particularly as wages and prices continue to rise. An excellent example of this sort of result on large loans is afforded in the study by the Royal Commission on Banking and Finance in Canada. The Commission noted that

. . . it is striking that a very low proportion of loans is made in the $1,000 to $1,500 range. This is not because there is little demand for loans over $1,000—about one-quarter all cash lending is in amounts over $1,500—but because the companies find the ½ of 1 per cent a month maximum rate allowed on balances in the $1,000 to $1,500 range barely covers their cost of funds and in fact involves them in losses after administrative and bad debt expenses.[12]

The Commission went on to recommend an increase in the rates permitted on loans in this bracket.[13]

GENERAL APPLICABILITY OF CEILINGS ON RATES

The effort to draft uniform consumer credit legislation raises the question whether rates on ceilings should be uniform among the several states. At present they are far from uniform. There is a tendency to argue that economic and demographic characteristics differ from state to state; hence, ceiling rates should differ as well. While there is certainly merit to the argument, it is equally applicable within states. The economic and demographic characteristics of consumers in the Michigan cities of Detroit and Ishpeming probably differ as widely as those of people in New Jersey and South Dakota. Within the city of Detroit there are probably equally wide variations. If one were to aim to fit ceilings precisely either to costs or to the credit standing of consumers, it would be necessary to design rate ceilings suitable for each loan office. This might be appropriate for a public utility, but not for the highly competitive business of cash lending.

The analysis in the latter part of Chapter IV indicates that at least the large companies allocate "a larger proportion of their funds to

[12] *Report of the Royal Commission on Banking and Finance.* Ottawa, 1964, p. 209.

[13] *Ibid.*, p. 562.

states where operating profits were higher, where the number of loans per office was larger, and where they were able to obtain a larger share of the market." Thus if ceilings on rates are unusually low in any given state, the strong tendency is to drive funds away from that state and into states that encourage cash lending to a broader segment of the market through a more favorable rate structure.[14] Thus our presumption is to favor relatively high ceilings which permit competition to establish rates below ceiling in locations where economically feasible. Tight, uniform ceilings would eliminate cash loans in some regions.

Even with a favorable uniform rate ceiling there will be pockets of high-risk consumers that cannot be provided credit, and there may be more pockets in some states than in others. However, these variations do not seem to provide grounds for varying the ceilings on rates from state to state. Lack of adequate credit standing reflects much more fundamental social and economic problems. If we assume a free economic system, with capital free to move across state lines, a uniform ceiling appears desirable, although more research on this point would be welcome.

UNANSWERED QUESTIONS

The actual formulation of a ceiling on consumer finance charges involves much more detailed work than has been indicated thus far. The rapid growth of various types of credit insurance raises the issue of how these charges are to be regulated. In some cases the use of certain kinds of property insurance has been abused by credit grantors. Charges for delinquencies, refinancing, and extensions must be limited. While such charges are included in the gross income studied in earlier chapters, their structure should not encourage cash lenders to develop financial arrangements that are harmful to consumers.

Finally, as indicated in the previous section, there is the problem of the consumer who is not entitled to credit at prevailing rates. As we raise rate ceilings on small loans, we enlarge the size of the market that can be served by legal lenders and we diminish the size of the market that can be served by illegal lenders. Hopefully, we set ceilings high enough so that the size of that market is too small to generate a large enough volume of loans to attract illegal lenders. But this will still require rate ceilings on small loans that leave some

[14] This effect is currently observable in eastern and southern states, where the low rates established by archaic usury laws are driving investment funds from these states to areas with higher permissable rates. *Wall Street Journal*, July 12, 1966.

consumers with no access to legal sources of credit. In all likelihood, the needs of the poor consumer—poor in an economic sense—cannot be met by uniform credit legislation. To attempt to do so would warp the legislation and quite possibly harm the interests of the great mass of consumers who can be served by consumer finance companies and other cash lenders. Through training and education consumers in pockets of poverty must be aided to gain sufficient credit stature so that they can receive credit at rates appropriate to the bulk of the market.

Ceilings on Size of Credit Extensions

The first draft of the Uniform Small Loan Law fifty years ago carried a ceiling of $300. If this were adjusted to today's consumer price levels, the ceiling should be about $900. However, even this adjustment is inadequate, since it accounts only for changes in price levels and not for the upward shift in incomes and changes in scale of living. Consequently, in states like New Jersey consumer finance companies are restricted by law to a smaller portion of the credit market than was permitted them in 1920.

States presently fix ceilings on the size of loans that may be made by licensed lenders at anywhere from $300 to an unlimited amount in South Carolina.[15] Our purpose in this section is to examine the evidence presented in the preceding chapters to see if this disparity in ceilings on amounts loaned is justified, or indeed if any such ceiling is warranted.

There are two basic methods of providing higher ceilings on size of loan. On the one hand, states might raise the ceilings of laws based on the Uniform Small Loan Act. This has the advantage of extending the various other protections found in those laws to a broader spectrum of the cash loan market. However, the detailed regulation appropriate to small loans is probably less necessary for large loans, where competition is generally more effective. On the other hand, states might enact ancillary loan laws providing for larger loans (and typically lower rates). While ancillary acts enable cash lenders to provide needed services to consumers, the complexity and diversity of regulation are necessarily increased. In some states, for example, a

[15] As noted earlier, a number of states having ceilings on "small loans" also have ancillary acts permitting larger loans.

consumer might obtain a loan of the same dollar amount under either of two different laws. It is this type of development, as well as the wide diversity of consumer credit legislation among the states, that led the National Conference of Commissioners on Uniform State Laws to undertake the drafting of uniform consumer credit legislation.

The analysis is complicated by the dual effect of small-loan laws side by side with ancillary laws. Where the sizes of loans covered by the laws overlap, there are discontinuities in applicable rate ceilings that lead companies to favor one law or the other in those areas.

REASONS FOR CEILING

The original small-loan ceiling of $300 was set to establish a classification of borrowers who needed the protection of the state against the abuses of illegal lenders. At a time when the average weekly income was about $15, it was believed that the $300 ceiling would include most legitimate cases of consumer credit. In more recent years the ceiling has also been viewed by some as a means of forcing consumer finance companies to serve borrowers of small amounts. In point of fact, the data developed in earlier chapters suggest that the economic impact of low ceilings is precisely opposite to that intended. Recall the finding that "states with $300 loan ceilings result in extremes of high gross income, high operating expense, high risk, and low net operating income per dollar of average loan outstanding." This is hardly a cost-profit picture that is likely to encourage consumer finance companies to open offices and offer credit to consumers wishing to borrow small amounts.

Not only do low ceilings discourage extension of loans to borrowers of small amounts but they encourage high-cost multiple loans. To illustrate, a New Jersey consumer needing $1,500 for twelve months might obtain three loans of $500 each and pay a finance charge of $214.32. Yet he could obtain the same sum for a charge of $137.84 in the adjoining state of Pennsylvania under its ancillary act, if he could qualify for the loan at the lower rate. Thus low ceilings on loans penalize those wishing to borrow small amounts because credit is restricted by high costs and low profits and penalizes those wishing large amounts by forcing them to pay the costs of multiple loans.

TRENDS IN LOAN CEILINGS

It was observed in the second chapter that the average size of outstanding personal loans at consumer finance companies has increased substantially over the years and "by nearly 30 per cent in the first five years of the 1960's." This has been a product of higher ceilings on loans in small loan statutes or in various ancillary acts. The record of this trend and data from other chapters may foretell the results of further increases in ceilings on loans, or their removal altogether.

The evidence implies that, while further increases in ceilings are desirable, the effect may not be as great as that produced by the changes that have already taken place. Much of the decline in gross income per $100 of loans outstanding has resulted from the application of graduated rate structures to larger and larger loans. In spite of rising prices and wages, consumer finance companies were able to spread their relatively (but not entirely) fixed costs per loan over the larger amounts outstanding so that operating expenses per $100 of average outstanding credit also fell. However, income fell faster than expenses, with the result that net operating income per $100 of outstandings declined. The increases in costs of borrowing in 1965–66 has squeezed profits available for owners even more than indicated in Table 5 of Chapter II.

While higher loan ceilings and ancillary acts have permitted consumer finance companies to expand their volume and, in a sense, to stave off a more painful cost-price squeeze, it seems unlikely that further increases in the ceiling will have the same effect. The analysis of the forty-eight companies in Chapter III shows that gross income per $100 of loans outstanding was lower by an average of $1.71 and operating expenses an average of $1.26 for each $100 increase in average loan size. While the inverse correlation of net operating profit to loan size was not statistically significant, the data do support the cost-price squeeze already noted in Chapter II. But now we must note the point made earlier in this chapter that costs per $100 of outstandings cannot be expected to decline indefinitely as loan size increases. When cost ratios level off in relation to average loan size, and gross income ratios do not, consumer finance companies could face a break-even point on large, as well as small, loans. In short, any increase in ceiling on size of loan must be accompanied by a leveling off of the ceiling on rates at some point in relation to size of loan. Otherwise, an increase in ceiling on size of loan will be only a matter of form. The squeeze between costs and ceilings on rates will prevent consumer finance companies from making large loans, just as it has in Canada on loans between $1,000 and $1,500. The disinclination of consumer finance companies to increase the average size of their loans, even with ceilings above $2,000 (Table 22, Chapter IV), implies that the cost-price squeeze may already be affecting the availability of large loans from consumer finance companies.[16]

[16] See also Comiskey, "Loan Cost Behavior," pp. 111–117.

amount outstanding, this appears to be a more appropriate measure of scale of operation.

By studying the behavior of these direct costs per loan in individual offices within four states, Comiskey found that the average direct cost per account decreased up to approximately 2,000 accounts per office. Beyond this point, unit costs increased in two of the states (curve A), and continued to decline, but at a decreasing rate, in two other states (curve B).[17]

Analysis of cost data alone is inadequate, since it abstracts from what happens to the revenue per account as the number of accounts per office increases. Thus the lowest point on the curve is not necessarily the optimal point at which a small-loan office should operate. This would be true only if the revenue per loan were constant, regardless of the number of loans per office. If the average revenue per account varies directly or inversely with the number of accounts per office, then the operations should not be determined solely by the minimum cost point.

Evidence from this study shows that revenues per loan are inversely related to the number of loans per office. As noted in Chapter III, "there is a significant inclination for companies with relatively high levels of loan-office activity to make comparatively small-size loans." Because of the graduated rate structure, it follows that gross income per $100 of loans outstanding is higher in loan offices with a large number of loans outstanding than in small-volume offices. In contrast, the gross income *per account* is likely to be lower the larger the number of loans per office. Chart 5 in Chapter III suggests that gross revenue per $100 of average balance outstanding amounts to $21 on loan balances averaging $600 and $28 on loans averaging $200. But this implies revenues *per loan* of $126 and $56, respectively. Thus gross

[17] *Ibid.*, pp. 117–122. The curves shown in Chart 25 are from his Figures 4–10 and 4–11, representing two of the four states. Unfortunately, the multiple correlation measure used in Chapter III failed to reveal a statistically significant relationship between operating costs per $100 of outstandings and the number of loans per office among 48 companies. The finding that operating earnings before interest and taxes are higher, the higher the number of loans per office is consistent with average cost curves similar to either A or B, depending upon the shape of the gross revenue curves. Moreover, the interpretation is obscured by interstate differences in operating conditions. The analysis of Chapter IV indicates that operating costs are lower, the larger the number of loans per office among states (Table 24). However, the measuring tool is not able to determine whether the cost curve is U-shaped or constantly downward-sloping.

revenue per account varies inversely with the number of accounts, because the average loan outstanding is smaller in large offices than in small offices.

The inverse correlation between revenues per account and number of accounts has two implications. First, the minimum-cost point does not represent the optimal level of operations for a loan office. Second, even with a declining direct-cost curve per account (curve B), a loan office may limit its expansion if the result of that expansion is the assumption of numbers of small loans offering relatively small revenues per account.

By careful study of costs and revenues of each small-loan office in a given market area, it is conceptually possible that a regulatory authority could apply C and A provisions to encourage offices to move closer to an optimal level of operations. If offices in a market area would otherwise operate below optimal levels, tightening of C and A provisions would restrict the number of offices and quite probably increase the number of loans per office. On the other hand the easing of C and A restraints would either maintain or move offices closer to an optimal level of operations and increase loan services in markets where there was excessive restraint of entry, as implied by the findings of Chapter IV.

While it is conceptually possible to support limited application of convenience and advantage provisions, there are some very practical objections. First, it would be difficult for the regulatory authority to develop and to interpret cost and revenue data for each office in a market area in order to determine the impact of permitting a new licensed lender to enter the market. The costs of this research would be considerable, both to the industry and to the regulatory body. Second, a trade-off is involved which may vary from office to office. Enforcement of convenience and advantage provisions may lower expenses for individual offices by increasing the number of accounts outstanding. But this same action tends to reduce the amount of legitimate loan service available, as shown in Chapter IV. An error in excessive restriction of entry may be substantial in terms of fewer services to consumers, as may be the case in the six states studied in Chapter IV. Third, even if restriction of entry through application of C and A provisions is "successful" in the sense that each office in a market area operates closer to its optimal level, this does not necessarily result in benefits to consumers in that market. Rate ceilings in a state are not varied for each market area. By restricting entry to any given market, the regulatory authority creates elements of monopoly power. Thus application of C and A provisions may grant monopoly profits to offices operating in low-risk markets rather than encourage price reductions to consumers.

Justification for C and A provisions is sometimes based on possible restrictions of undesirable competitive practices. Whether these can be controlled directly rather than by restricting competition is open to question.[18] However, when pleas are made to constrain competition in order to create a more healthy market, we should recall the adage of the devout capitalist: "It is unfair competition for thee to compete with me, but healthy competition for me to compete with thee."

Regardless of the outcome of the dispute on convenience and advantage provisions, the analysis developed in the first chapter supports less need for the detailed restrictions and regulations formulated since 1916. The general growth of significant competition in the making of loans to consumers, especially large loans, requires less legal restriction on operations. There was once good reason to rely heavily on the regulation of law, rather than competition. The rapid growth of alternative sources of credit, the increased sophistication of consumers, and proposed time-rate disclosure of finance charges suggest a need for an intensive review of the detailed regulations incorporated in the present small-loan laws and regulations. To the extent that these regulations raise costs of operations and restrict the freedom of consumer finance companies to compete without providing significant benefits or protections to consumers, the regulations should probably be eased. However, as observed in Chapter IV, it is also appropriate to "bring about both a more consistent regulatory atmosphere and more uniform protection to an enlarged group of borrowers." This aim can be achieved by replacing the present patchwork of small-loan laws and ancillary acts with a Uniform Consumer Credit Code.

---

[18] A distinction should be made between a restriction on licensing entry based upon convenience and advantage and a requirement that before granting a license the Commissioner find "that the financial responsibility, experience, character and general fitness of the applicant are such as to command the confidence of the public and to warrant belief that the business will be operated lawfully, honestly, fairly, and efficiently" (Seventh Draft of the Uniform Small Loan Law). Among other objectives such requirements are designed to prevent the underworld from entering the small-loan business. If properly administered with adequate provisions for prompt denials and appeals, such a provision appears to be desirable.

Summary

This study has shed light on three main areas of regulation of consumer finance companies by the states. With respect to the general level of ceilings on rates, the analysis shows that present levels of ceilings have not permitted excessive profits. Indeed, there are implications that under the present levels of rate ceilings profits are being squeezed between rising costs and lower operating revenues per $100 of loans outstanding. While this will ultimately lead consumer finance companies to restrict their lending activities, no general rule for the proper level of rate ceilings can be given. This depends upon one's view of the proportion of consumers that should be "admitted" to the legal market for cash loans in relation to those that should forgo their use of credit, turn to illegal lenders, or become subjects for economic rehabilitation, perhaps for charity. The data indicate that it is appropriate to design an augmented rate ceiling available only to closely regulated lenders that declines with the amount of the loan. At some point this ceiling should level off to the general rate ceiling available to all lenders. The exact slope of the augmented rate ceiling is a matter of economics, philosophy, and politics. If the slope is too steep, many small, possibly multiple, loans will be encouraged, and this may cause an uneconomic allocation of resources. In contrast, if the slope is too gradual, cash lenders will be discouraged from serving the demand for small loans.

There appears to be sound reason for increasing or, better, eliminating the ceilings on the amounts that can be loaned to each consumer. The opportunity to convert several small, expensive loans into a large loan at a lower rate and the higher earnings available on large loans up to a point should encourage better credit service to all borrowers. Credit grantors should be permitted to set their own limits, depending upon the credit standing of the applicant and the skill of the loan officer.

Finally, we were able to shed no brilliant light on the controversy over convience and advantage provisions in state small-loan laws. However, data suggest that convenience and advantage provisions reduce the level of loan services to consumers, though possibly providing an opportunity for reduction in costs to other consumers. In particular, the evidence of Chapter IV places the burden of proof on those who wish to restrict competition. With the great changes that have taken place in the consumer credit field since 1916, there is considerable reason to believe that a lightening of the detailed restrictions on the operations of consumer finance companies is in order.

Thus, as a general rule, appropriate relaxation of legal constraints upon the granting of loans under small-loan statutes can be expected to increase loan services. Such relaxation may take the form of increasing permissible rates of charge or altering the rate ceiling structure in states that have both relatively low rates and low provision of loan service. Or it might also take the form of increasing permissible loan ceilings. Finally, an expansion of "legal" loan services should follow relaxation of restraints on entry in states where population per office is high. Regardless of any relaxation of ceilings on rates and size of loan or any provision for greater freedom of entry, suitable protection for all borrowers should be provided.

Appendix 1

Description of Nine-Company Consumer Finance Sample and of Adjustments in Data

The sample and procedures used in adjusting the data for Chapter II of this study were similar to those used in an earlier study conducted for the National Bureau of Economic Research.[1] Two types of adjustments had to be made in the information obtained from the sample companies. First, statement data had to be adjusted to conform to the conceptual framework used in the study. Second, estimates of selected items had to be made when the accounting records of the company could not provide the necessary detail.

All income and expense data for the sample companies were classified into three groups: (1) those associated with consumer credit activities, (2) those associated with all other earning activities, and (3) those associated with obtaining funds, either equity or nonequity. Cost accounting data were used to establish the proper classification except in a few cases where estimates had to be made.

The cost of funds, both equity and nonequity, and provision for income taxes were further allocated to consumer credit and other activities by the following rules: (1) The costs of nonequity funds were distributed according to the proportion of average earning assets used in these activities. (2) Income taxes and cost of equity funds were distributed according to the proportion of net operating income obtained from these activities. The details of the adjustments in individual company data are presented in the following discussion.

The samples used in the study were necessarily small because only relatively few companies could supply the detail needed and because of the elaborate processing of the data that was required. The results of the study do not necessarily represent all companies, but are

[1] Paul F. Smith, *Consumer Credit Costs, 1949–59*, Princeton, 1964.

163

intended merely to present data on costs in a standard accounting framework.

The following consumer finance companies supplied the information used in the study: American Investment Company, Beneficial Finance Company, Family Finance Corporation, Household Finance Corporation, Credithrift Financial Corporation, Liberty Loan Corporation, Merchants Acceptance Corporation, Seaboard Finance Company, State Loan & Finance Corporation.

These nine companies held $3.1 billion in consumer receivables at the end of 1964 and accounted for 66 per cent of the loans held by all consumer finance companies and 50 per cent of the receivables of all personal finance companies. The companies are among the largest in operation. All but one of them had more than $100 million in receivables and had more than 100 branch offices. A comparison of some of their principal characteristics with estimates for all personal finance companies based on a survey conducted in 1964 is shown in Appendix Table 1.

Although all of the companies in this group engaged primarily in making loans under the state small-loan laws, a few of them held substantial amounts of purchased instalment contracts secured either by automobiles or other durable goods. Their other activities, limited primarily to insurance and wholesale financing of dealer inventories, represented a relatively small part of the total activities when measured either by income received or funds invested.

Since the information available from the accounting records of these companies differed in form of presentation and in composition, some rearrangement in the data was necessary to obtain uniformity. Estimates were also necessary in some cases to fill gaps in accounting information. The following list describes the principal adjustments that were made in the data to adapt the information for use in the study. The procedures used in making these adjustments and estimating missing data necessarily varied from company to company, depending upon circumstances.

1. Reserves for bad-debt losses were added to the outstanding amount of receivables in cases where they had been subtracted in the financial statements of the reporting companies. Total assets were increased accordingly and the amount of reserves was included in the equity of the company.

2. Unearned discount was included in gross receivables, but was deducted to obtain net figures and total assets.

3. The current portion of debentures and other long-term debt was

APPENDIX TABLE 1

Comparison of Nine-Company Consumer Finance Sample with All
Personal Finance Companies, End of 1964

Item	All Personal Finance Companies[a]		Nine Sample Companies		Sample as Percentage of Total
	Million Dollars	Per Cent	Million Dollars	Per Cent	
Number of companies	2,493	—	9	—	0.4
Principal sources and uses of funds					
Consumer receivables, total					
Gross	7,498	90.1	—	—	—
Less: Unearned income[b]	(841)	10.1	—	—	—
Net	6,657	80.0	3,361	85.6	50.5
Personal loans[c]	6,479	77.8	3,069	78.2	—
Other consumer receivables[c]	1,019	12.2	292	7.4	—
Other earning assets	975	11.7	278	7.1	28.5
Other assets	692	8.3	286	7.3	41.3
Total sources and uses	8,324	100.0	3,925[d]	100.0	47.2
Nonequity sources	6,408	77.0	2,947	75.1	46.0
Equity sources[e]	1,916	23.0	978	24.9	51.0

[a] Based on preliminary unpublished data supplied by the staff of Board of Governors of the Federal Reserve System from a survey of finance companies. Some industrial loan companies are included as personal finance companies that are not included in figures for consumer finance companies as regularly published by the Board.

[b] Figure for unearned income is the total for all types of receivables and may include a small amount on nonconsumer receivables which are included in "other earning assets."

[c] Figures for all personal finance companies include unearned income. Those for the nine sample companies exclude unearned income.

[d] Includes figures for the Canadian subsidiaries of some of the nine companies.

[e] Includes reserves for losses on loans.

removed from figures for short-term debt and was included with long-term debt.

4. Estimates of the administrative costs of obtaining funds were made for each company on the basis of cost studies available for one company. The amount of these costs was deducted from operating cost and included with the cost of nonequity funds.

5. Where free life insurance was extended to borrowers, its cost was deducted from gross income and from expenses.

6. Estimates of the cost of insurance operations were made for companies that did not have separate insurance subsidiaries and could not provide separate cost figures. These costs were included in the nonconsumer credit operating costs.

7. Estimates of the cost of wholesale financing were made on the basis of cost data from sales finance companies. These costs were included as nonconsumer credit operating expenses.

Appendix 2

Consumer Finance Rate

and

Regulation Chart

COMPILED BY

National Consumer Finance Association
1000 Sixteenth Street, N. W., Washington, D. C. 20036

December 1, 1964

CONSUMER FINANCE RATE AND REGULATION CHART

Editors warning: National Consumer Finance Association has compiled this chart on the basis of the Consumer Finance and other loan laws referred to, and legal opinions of lawyers who are personally familiar with the laws in the different states. It was necessary to over-simplify and to generalize the statutes and legal opinions in order to present the information in this abbreviated chart form. Each NCFA member should consult his own counsel for each state statute and detail shown on this chart. For example, the convenience and advantage (C&A) clauses are generally similar in each state law but administrative interpretations of these clauses differ markedly among the states. In some states, insurance practices vary from company to company, depending on the opinion of different counsel and the organization of the company. Pre-computation and dollar add-on laws also result in varying practices among the states and companies as to rebate, default, and deferment charges. There are varying statutory and official administrative rules as to advertising, other business, security, maturities, record keeping, disclosures to customers and other matters.

State	Maximum Rate and Loan Size (monthly rate unless otherwise stated)	Maximum Maturity	Precomputation, Discount or Dollar Add-on	Default Charges	C & A Clause	Credit Insurance Life rate—per $100 per year. Disability rate—per $100 for indicated term (unless otherwise stated)	Other Laws (under which consumer finance licensees frequently operate)
Alabama	3–2% @ $200 to $300; $1 per $5 of loans not exceeding $75	25 months	Precomputation	Yes	Yes	Life, 75¢, on loans above $100	Installment Loan Act: 6% per annum add-on; no max. amount or maturity
Alaska	4–2½% @ $300, 2% @ $600 to $1,000; 5% on loans not exceeding $50; default fee of $3	No max. maturity	None	Yes	Yes	Life, premiums actually paid out	———
Arizona	3–2% @ $300, 1% @ $600 to $1,000	24½ months	Precomputation	Yes	No	Life and Disability, NAIC	Installment Loan Act: 8% per annum add-on to $1,000, 6% on any excess to $3,500; no max. maturity
California	2½–2% @ $200 (2% if security insured), ⅚% @ $500 to $5,000; no. max. above $5,000	24 months	Precomputation	Yes	No	Life, 68¢	———
Canada	2–1% @ $300, ½% @ $1,000 to $1,500; 1% after maturity and after 20 or 30 months	20 months to $500; 30 months over $500	None	—	—	Life, 50¢ by administrative interpretation	General Interest Law: No limit on rate above $1,500
Colorado	3–1½% @$300, 1% @ $500 to $1,500	No max. maturity	Precomputation	Yes	No	Life and Disability, insurance law	1913 Money Lenders Act: 2% per month on loans over $1,500; no max. amount or maturity
Connecticut	$17–$9 a year per $100 @ $300 to $1,000 add-on; 12% a yr. after deferred maximum maturity	24½ months	Add-on	Yes	Yes	Life, 50¢ or actual cost if less	———

Note: "Precomputation" means that monthly rate may be precomputed on scheduled monthly balances instead of actual balances. "Add-on" and "Discount" rates are for the contract period without regard to installment payments. Add-on is computed on and added to the original amount lent. Discount is computed on and deducted from the face amount of the note. In the Credit Insurance column, "NAIC" refers to statutes which give Insurance Commissioners some control of credit insurance premiums and which are based on a model bill of the National Association of Insurance Commissioners.

State	Maximum Rate and Loan Size (monthly rate unless otherwise stated)	Maximum Maturity	Precomputation, Discount or Dollar Add-on	Default Charges	C & A Clause	*Credit Insurance* Life rate—per $100 per year. Disability rate—per $100 for indicated term (unless otherwise stated)	Other Laws (under which consumer finance licensees frequently operate)
Delaware	6% a year discount; 2% service fee; 5% fine; various limitations; industrial law; loan size based on capital and surplus	36 months	Discount and fee	Yes	No	——	——
Florida	3–2% @ $300 to $600; 10% a year 12 months after maturity	24 months	None	—	Yes	Life and Disability, NAIC	Discount Act: $10 a year per $100 add-on plus 20¢ per $25 to $600 limited to $2.40 per month; 24 months max.
Georgia	8% a year, to $2,500 discount for 18 months, add-on for longer maturities; fee of 8% of first $600 and 4% of excess.	24 months	Discount and fee	Yes	Yes	Life, $1.00 reducing balance, $2 level term. Disability (3 day retro.) ; $3.60 per annum per $5 monthly benefit; (7 day retro.) : $2.10 per annum per $5 monthly benefit	——
Hawaii	3½–2½% @ $100 to $300	20 months	None	—	Yes	Life, premiums actually paid out	Industrial Loan Act: 12% per annum discount for first 18 months, 9% per annum for next 12 months, 6% per annum for next 12 months, 3% per annum for remaining months to 48 months; also delinquency and other charges; no max. amount
Idaho	3–2% @ $300, 1% @ $500 to $1,000	No max. maturity	Precomputation	Yes	Yes	No	——
Illinois	3–2% @ $150, 1% @ $300 to $800	Regulation prohibits advertising maturity over 24 months	Precomputation	Yes	Yes	NAIC. Life, 75¢— Disability (14 day retro.) : $2.20—12 months, $3.00—24 months, $4.00—36 months	Installment Loan Act: Annual discount rates ranging from 8½% for maturities up to 30 months down to 7.09% for 58 to 61 months. Loans over $800 to $5,000 excluding discount. General Interest Act: 7% per annum add-on to $7,500; 61 months max. maturity

State	Maximum Rate and Loan Size (monthly rate unless otherwise stated)	Maximum Maturity	Precomputation, Discount or Dollar Add-on	Default Charges	C & A Clause	*Credit Insurance* Life rate—per $100 per year. Disability rate—per $100 for indicated term (unless otherwise stated)	Other Laws (under which consumer finance licensees frequently operate)
Indiana	3–2% @ $150, 1½% @ $300 to $1,000	No max. maturity	None	—	No	NAIC. Life, 75¢ Disability (14 day retro.): $2.20—12 months, $3.00—24 months, $3.80—36 months	Industrial Loan Act: 1½% per month; precomputation with default charge; max. 10% of capital; no max. maturity; special provisions for real estate loans
Iowa	3–2% @ $150, 1½% @ $300 to $500	No max. maturity	None	—	Yes	Life, 1% of "amount repayable." Disability (14 day retro.): 2.2%—12 months, 3%—24 months of total amount repayable. Banking Board regulation	Morris Plan method: Fragmentary law originally a tax statute. No max. amount or maturity
Kansas	3–⅝% @ $300 to $2,100; 10% a year 6 months after maturity	30 months	Precomputation	No	No	Life and Disability, above $300	————
Kentucky	3–2% @ $150, 1% @ $600 to $800; or add-on rates, $20–$15 a year per $100 @ $150, $11 @ $600 to $800	25 months	Add-on	Yes	Yes	Life, premium reasonable in relation to death benefit	Industrial Loan Act: 6% per annum discount plus fee $1 per $50 or fraction thereof to $2,000; 5% discount for excess to $5,000. Max. maturity 3 years, 32 days
Louisiana	3½–2½% @ $150 to $300; 8% a year 1 yr. after maturity	No max. maturity	None	—	Yes	Life, $1 (by regulation)	Usury Law Provision: No limit over $300 as to interest included in face of loan note; no max. maturity
Maine	3–2½% @ $150, 1½% @ $300 to $2,500; 25¢ minimum	No max. maturity	None	—	No	NAIC. Life, 64¢. Disability (14 day retro.): $1.93—6 months, $2.37—12 months, $2.84—24 months, $3.20—36 months,	General Interest Law: No limit on rate over $2,500
Maryland	3% to $300	No max. maturity	None	—	Yes	Life, no commissions to licensee	Industrial Finance Law: 6% per annum discount plus fee of $4 or 4% up to $500, and $20 or 2% of face of any note exceeding $500; $1,500 max. face of note

State	Maximum Rate and Loan Size (monthly rate unless otherwise stated)	Maximum Maturity	Precomputation, Discount or Dollar Add-on	Default Charges	C & A Clause	Credit Insurance Life rate—per $100 per year. Disability rate—per $100 for indicated term (unless otherwise stated)	Other Laws (under which consumer finance licensees frequently operate)
Massachusetts	2½–2% @ $200, 1¾% @ $600, ¾% @ $1,000 to $3,000; 6% a year 1 year after maturity	No max. maturity	Precomputation	Yes	Not in law but by regulation	Life, 50¢, insurance law	General Interest Law: No limit on rate over $3,000 except for certain home mortgage loans
Michigan	2½–1¼% @ $300 to $1,000	No max. maturity	None	—	Yes	NAIC. Life, 60¢	———
Minnesota	2¾–1½% @ $300 to $600	24½ months (by regulation)	Precomputation	Yes	Yes	Life. Disability (14 day retro.)	Industrial Loan Act: 8% per annum discount plus fee of $1 per each $50 or fraction to $500 and 1% of excess, but $15 max.; max. amount 5% of paid-in capital and surplus (10% if secured); 36 months max. maturity
Mississippi	Broker's service charge and lender's interest not to exceed 2% per month add-on on loans of $100 or more, graduated scale for smaller loans; no max. amount	No max. maturity over $100	Add-on	No	No	Life, $1. Disability (14 day retro.): $2.20—12 months, $3.00—24 months, $3.80—36 months (by regulation)	———
Missouri	2.218% to $500; 8% a year on remainder	No max. maturity	Precomputation	No	No	Life	———
Montana	$20–$16 a year per $100 @ $300, $12 @ $500 to $1,000 add-on; special rate for loans up to $90	21 months to $300; 25 months over $300; special schedule on loans of $90 or less	Add-on	Yes	No	No	———
Nebraska	2½–2% @ $300, 1½% @ $500, 1% @ $1,000 to $3,000	36 months	Precomputation	Yes	Yes	NAIC. Life, 75¢. Disability (14 day retro.): $2.20—12 months, $3.00—24 months, $3.80—36 months	———
Nevada	9–8% a year @ $1,000 to $2,500 plus monthly fee of 1¢ per $1 to $200 and ½¢ per $1 from $200 to $400 all add-on	24 months	Add-on	Yes	Yes	Life, 50¢ (by regulation)	———

State	Maximum Rate and Loan Size (monthly rate unless otherwise stated)	Maximum Maturity	Precomputation, Discount or Dollar Add-on	Default Charges	C & A Clause	*Credit Insurance* Life rate—per $100 per year. Disability rate—per $100 for indicated term (unless otherwise stated)	Other Laws (under which consumer finance licensees frequently operate)
New Hampshire	$16–$12 a year per $100 @ $600 to $1,500 add-on; 6% a year 6 months after maturity	24 months	Add-on	Yes	No	NAIC. Life, 64¢	General Interest Law: No limit on rate above $1,500 except for certain home mortgage loans
New Jersey	2½–½% @ $300 to $500	24 months by regulation	None	—	Yes	NAIC. Life, 44¢–64¢ depending on outstandings	——
New Mexico	3–2½% @ $150, 1% @ $300 to $1,000; 10% a year 1 year after maturity and in certain other cases	No max. maturity	Precomputation	Yes	Yes	NAIC. Life, 75¢. Disability (14 day retro.): $2.35—12 months, $3.25—24 months, $4.15—36 months	——
New York	2½–2% @ $100, ¾% @ $300 to $800	24½ months by regulation	Precomputation	Yes	Yes	Life, rate approved by Insurance Superintendent	——
North Carolina	$20–$18 a year per $100 @ $100, $15 @ $200 to $300, $6 @ $300 to $600 add-on; 6% a year after maturity; $1 per $5 of loans not exceeding $75	25 months	Add-on	Yes	Yes	Life, level term permitted. Disability (14 day retro.): $2.35—12 months	——
North Dakota	2½–2% @ $250, 1¾% at $500 to $750, 1½% @ $750 to $1,000	24½ months	Precomputation but defective	Yes	No	Life and Disability	——
Ohio	$16–$9 a year per $100 @ $500, $7 @ $1,000 to $2,000 add-on; or equivalent simple interest rates	25½ months to $1,000, 37½ months over $1,000	Add-on	Yes	Yes	Life, rate filed with and not disapproved by Insurance Superintendent	——
Oklahoma	10% a year plus service charges not exceeding an initial 5% and monthly 2% but not more than $2, subject to various limitations to $300	20 months	None	—	Yes	——	The Certificate Plan (by court decision) 10% discount for 1 year; add-on for longer term; common law fees; no max. loan size or maturity
Oregon	3–2% @ $300, 1% @ $500 to $1,500	None	None	—	Yes	Life, 60¢	Industrial Loan Co. Act: 10% per annum discount plus 3% fee (minimum fee $3); max. loan, 5% of net worth; max. maturity, 18 months unsecured and 24 months when secured by chattels

State	Maximum Rate and Loan Size (monthly rate unless otherwise stated)	Maximum Maturity	Precomputation, Discount or Dollar Add-on	Default Charges	C & A Clause	*Credit Insurance* Life rate—per $100 per year. Disability rate—per $100 for indicated term (unless otherwise stated)	Other Laws (under which consumer finance licensees frequently operate)
Pennsylvania	3–2% @ $150, 1% @ $300 to $600, 6% a year after 24 months	24 months	None	—	Yes	Life, 60¢ (group); $1 (individual). NAIC and Banking Department regulation	Consumer Discount Company Act: 7½% per annum discount for 36 months, 6% for remaining period, plus max. fee of $15 ($1 for each $50 or fraction); 1½% per month for default or deferment; $3,500 max. size; max. maturity 4 yrs. and 15 days
Rhode Island	3% to $300	21 months by regulation	None	—	Yes	NAIC. Life, 75¢. Disability (14 day retro.): $2.49—12 months, $2.96—24 months, $3.51—36 months	General Interest Law: 30% per annum above $300; no max. amount or maturity
South Carolina	Initial Charge, 6% of cash advance plus 6% per annum to $200; $1.75 per month expense fee on loans $100 or over; 7% per annum on portion over $200; no max. loan size	24 months	Add-on	Yes	Yes	Life and Disability	——
South Dakota	3–¾% @ $300 to $2,500; $2 minimum; 8% a year, 6 months after maturity	24½ months to $1,000; 36½ months over $1,000	Precomputation	Yes	No	Life and Disability over $300	
Tennessee	½% to $300; monthly fee not exceeding 1%	None	None	—	No	No	Industrial Loan Act: 6% per annum discount plus 4% fee; max. amount 10% of capital and surplus; max. maturity 3 years
Texas	$19–$16 a year per $100 @ $100, $13 @ $200, $11 @ $300, $9 @ $500, $7 @ $1,000 to $1,500 add-on; special rate for loans up to $100	37 months	Add-on	Yes	No	NAIC. Life, 90¢ to $700; 80¢ for larger coverage. Disability (14 day retro.): Coverage to $700: $2.60—12 months, $3.50—24 months, $4.45—36 months; Coverage over $700: $2.25—12 months, $3.05—24 months, $3.85—36 months.	——

State	Maximum Rate and Loan Size (monthly rate unless otherwise stated)	Maximum Maturity	Precomputation, Discount or Dollar Add-on	Default Charges	C & A Clause	*Credit Insurance* Life rate—per $100 per year. Disability rate—per $100 for indicated term (unless otherwise stated)	Other Laws (under which consumer finance licensees frequently operate)
Utah	3–1% @ $300 to $600	21 months to $300; 25 months over $300	None	—	Yes	Life and Disability, NAIC	Industrial Loan Act: 1% per month add-on to $2,000, ¾% on excess to $5,000; plus 2% fee ($2 minimum and $20 max.); max. maturity 37 months
Vermont	2½–2¼% @ $125, 1% @ $300 to $600	No max. maturity	Precomputation	—	Yes	Life, Insurance Law	————
Virginia	2½–1½% @ $300 to $600; 6% a year after 23 months and in certain other cases	21 months	None	—	Yes	Life and Disability	————
Washington	3–1½% @ $300, 1% @ $500 to $1,000; $1 minimum	25½ months	Precomputation	Yes	Yes	Life, 60¢	Industrial Loan Co. Law: 10% per annum discount plus 2% fee ($2 minimum fee) and 50¢ per month; max. loan 2% of paid-in capital and surplus; max. maturity, 2 years
West Virginia	3–2% @ $200, 1½% @ $600 to $800; or add-on rates, $19–$16 a year per $100 @ $200, $12 @ $600 to $800	24½ months to $300; 30½ months over $300 by regulation	Add-on	Yes	Yes	Life	Industrial Loan Act: 6% discount plus fees of $1 per $50; max. amount 10% of paid-up capital and surplus; max. maturity 2 years
Wisconsin	2½–2% @ $100, 1% @ $200 to $300	20 months by regulation	None	—	Yes	No	Sec. 115.09: 8% per annum discount on first $300, 7% on excess; 2% fee not exceeding $20; Max. proceeds, $2,000; 30½ months max. maturity
Wyoming	3½–2½% @ $150; 1% @ $300 to $1,000; plus $1 fee on loans of $50 or less: $1 recording fee	No max. maturity	None	—	No	Life and Disability, NAIC	————

Index

Acquisition costs, 21, 22
Advertising costs, 38, 39, 40, 62, 148
  finance charges and, 51–52
  profit rates and, 53
Alabama, 93–95, 97, 100, 108–110,
  118, 147
American Association of Small Loan
  Brokers, 13
American Bar Association, 27
American Investment Company, 90, 114
*Analysis of the Licensed Lender In-
  dustry, New York State, 1945–57,*
  99n
Ancillary laws, 87, 88–89, 138, 153–155
Applications for loans, 18–19
  cost of investigations, 22, 62, 150
  rejections, 18–19, 21–23, 25, 145
Arizona, 91n, 101, 108–109, 118–119
Assets
  in cash and bank balances, 30, 42–43
  distribution of, 42–43
  earning, 42
  effective use of total resources, 43–44
  nonearning, 42–43
  ratio of net operating income to
    total, 45–47
  return on total assets, 45–47
Automobile credit, 1, 7, 14, 16–17
Average loan size, 92–93
  gross-income ratio and, 102
  loan ceilings and, 100–101
  net operating income ratios and, 104
  operating expense ratios and, 103
  ranking by states, 108–109

Bad-debt ratio, 91, 92, 93, 96–97, 115–
  116
  gross-income ratios and, 99, 101–102
  net-operating income ratio and, 104
  operating-expense ratios and, 103
Bankruptcies, personal, 25–27, 139
Banks
  balances, 42, 43–44
  borrowing from, 43–44, 47
  profits, 19, 142

See also Commercial banks
Beneficial Finance Company, 90, 114
Borrowed funds, cost of, 121–136
  burden coverages, 122–125
  cash flows, 122
  commercial paper, 125, 128, 130–131
  compensating balance requirements,
    123n
  debt composition and, 135–136
  degree of leverage, 121, 122, 133, 134
  direct placements, 127
  discount rate, 133
  effect of company size, 121–126,
    134–135
    on costs, 123–125, 129
    long-term debt, 129–130, 135–
      136
    nonsubordinated long-term debt,
      126
    short-term borrowings, 125, 127,
      129–130
  equity funds, 44
  factors affecting, 122–123
  financial advantages in using, 47–49
  growth in demand for funds, 121
  interest costs, effect of, 47–49, 62,
    131–135
  liabilities, composition of, 125–133
    term structure of, 134–135
  negotiated borrowings, 122, 125
  prime bank rate and commercial
    paper rate, 131–133
  private placements, 127
  ratio of debt to equity, 49, 50
  ratio of nonequity to equity funds,
    48–49
  risk-bearing base, 122, 128, 130
  sample and data, 121
  senior long-term debt, 122, 125–126,
    129–130, 133, 135–136
  short-term financing, 125, 129–133,
    135
  subordinated debt, 126, 128, 129
  term structure, 134–135

175

Borrowers
  counseling, 18, 25–27
  credit analysis of, 18
  family incomes of, 18
  high-risk, 17
Brookings Institution, 27n
Burden coverage, 122–125
  definition, 123n
  cost of borrowing and, 123–125
Business loans, 55, 69, 77–80

Capital Finance Company, 26n
Captive finance companies, 122, 134
Cash flows, 122
Ceilings
  finance charges, *see* Finance charges,
    ceilings
  rates, *see* Rate ceilings
Charge-offs, 22–24, 144
  ratio to loans outstanding, 61n, 62,
    67
  reserves for, 24
  trends, 39
Collateral, security interest in, 150
Collections, 23
  costs of, 21, 26
  by loan sharks, 12–13
Comiskey, Eugene E., 149–150, 155n,
  156, 158
Commercial banks, 2, 13, 16, 137, 139
  competition and diversification, 15,
    30
  consumer instalment credit, 7–11, 14
  credit standards, 23
  finance charges, 15, 20–21
  functions, 13–14
  interest rates, 15
  personal cash loans, 7–8, 10
  profit ratios, compared to consumer
    finance companies, 21, 142–143
  short-term borrowing form, 125, 127,
    130–133
  size of loans, 15
Commercial paper
  market, 130–131
  rates, 130–131
    compared to prime bank rate, 131–
      132
  requirements for flotations, 131
  for short-term needs, 129, 130–133
Competition for consumer credit, 14–
  17, 30, 122, 137, 139–140

convenience and advantage clauses,
  effect of, 160
credit standards and, 25–26, 160
Connecticut, 101, 108–109, 111, 113,
  118–119
Consumer finance companies, 1–27
  collection policies, 23
  commercial banks compared with,
    21, 142–143
  commercial financing by, 16
  competition and diversification, 14–
    17, 30, 122, 137
    for larger loans, 139–140
  credit unions compared with, 14, 21
  definition, 2
  functions, 13–14
  growth and development, 13, 29–30
  laws and regulations, 12–13
  lenders of last resort, 11, 23, 25, 147
  need for, 12
  operating procedures, 30, 89, 114–
    120
  personal cash loans, 11, 14, 16
  risk management, 22–24
Consumer finance industry, 2–6
  comparison of companies with high-
    est and lowest charges, 50–52
  comparison of companies with high-
    est and lowest profit rates, 52–
    53
  cost differences, 19–21
  costs and earnings, study of, 55–86
  effect of rate ceilings on, 145–147
  factors affecting, 17–19
  functions, 13–14
  growth of, 13, 29–30
  objectives, 2
  related earning activities, 41–43
  return on total assets, 45–47
Consumer instalment credit, 1–11, 145
  amount outstanding, 2, 4, 6, 7–11
    compared to disposable personal
      income, 3–6, 18–19
    gross national product and, 3–6
    net public and private debt and,
      3–6
    percentage distribution by holder,
      9
  classes of, 1, 7
  cost of, 18
  definition, 1
  growing demand for, 2–6
  historical background, 11–13
  personal cash loans, 1, 7–9, 11–13

Consumer receivables, 2, 31–36, 61n
  components of finance charges on, 38
  expansion of, 29–30
  factors in return on, 32
  gross income on, 31–36
  return on, 31–36, 45
Convenience and advantage clauses, 88,
    96n, 103–104, 111–114, 156–161
  controversy over, 160–161
  definition, 88n
  economic analysis, 157–158
  effect on expense ratios, 114
  effect on level of operations, 159
  effect on loan services, 112–114, 161
  importance of, 157–158, 160
  relation to fixed assets, 156–160
  restraint of entry under, 112–114,
    156–160
  restrictions on competition, 160
  trends, 160, 161–162
Costs of consumer finance companies
  acquisition, 21, 22
  borrowed funds, *see* Borrowed funds
  collection, 21, 26
  differences among companies, 100–
    104
  direct, 149–150
    average unit cost curves, 157–158
  expense ratios in thirty states, 100–
    104
  factors affecting, 17–19, 55–58, 144
  fixed, 148
  of nonequity funds, 47
  nonoperating, *see* Nonoperating costs
  operating, *see* Operating costs
  per loan, 20, 56–57
  risks assumed by lender, 18–19, 56
  salary, 37–38, 40, 62
  of services, 17–19
  size of loans and, 55–57
  study of earnings and, 55–86
    effect of company characteristics,
      56–57, 63–64
Cottle, Sidney, 143n
Counseling services, 17, 18n, 25–27
  community, 25–26
  to lessen bankruptcies, 25–26
Credit standards, 18, 21
  consumer finance companies, 18, 20–
    22
  effect on risk management, 22–24
Credit unions, 2, 137
  compared to consumer finance com-
    panies, 14, 21

competition and diversification, 15,
    30
consumer instalment credit held by,
    7–11
finance charges, 20–21
functions, 13–14
interest rates, 15
losses, 24
nonoperating costs, 20
operating costs, 20
personal cash loans, 7–8, 14
size of loans, 15

Dauer, Ernst A., 8n
Dealers
  participation in finance charge, 51
  reserves, 44
Debts
  ratio of debt to equity, 30, 49, 50,
    146n
  senior long-term, 44, 122, 125–126,
    129–130, 133
  short-term, 44, 125, 129, 130–133,
    135
  subordinated, 44, 126, 128, 129
Deficiency judgments, 139
Delinquencies, 21, 152
Diversification, 14–17, 122
  consumer finance companies, 16–17
Dolphin, Robert, Jr., 25n, 26n

Earning assets, *see* Assets, earning
Earnings
  from related activities, 41–43
  study of industry costs and, 55–86
  trends, 45–47
    See also Profits
"EBIT" (earnings before interest and
    taxes), 63n, 71–74, 85
  ratios, 77–81, 85–86
Economic activity, effect on consumer
    instalment credit, 3, 6
Economic Report of the President, 4n,
    5n, 6n, 19, 142
Education, consumer, 25, 27, 138, 153
Equity funds
  cost of, 19, 38, 41
  ratio of debt to, 30, 49
  ratio of net profit to, 30, 142
  ratio of nonequity funds to, 48–49
  return on, 30, 51, 52
  sources of, 44
Expenses, operating, *see* Operating
    costs

Extensions of consumer credit, 25–27
  ceilings on size of, 152–154
  charges for, 152

Federal Reserve System, Board of
  Governors, 1, 2–3
Finance charges, 13, 139–153
  ceilings on, 15, 138, 139–153
    effect on consumers, 142–145
    effect on industry structure, 145–
     147
    level of, 142–147
    state legislation, 152–153
  comparison of companies with high-
    est and lowest, 50–52
  components of, 38
  differences among consumer credit
    institutions, 19–21
  factors affecting, 20–21
  graduated rate structure, 155
  on "higher-risk" loans, 15–16, 18
  on large loans, 146–147, 155
  need for reasonable profit, 142–143
  need for re-evaluation of, 138, 139–
    153
  operating costs and, 21, 51, 147–148
  on personal loans, 13
  question of uniform, 151–152
  related to size of loan, 148–151
  relationship to cost of services, 21,
    143–144, 146
  rules of disclosure, 138, 160
  state legislation, 15, 139–140, 152–
    153
  trends, 35, 152–153
Florida, 100, 108–109, 113, 118–119
Follow-up or supervision of loans, 23
"Forbearance" charges, 140
Funds
  cost of borrowing, 30, 48, 121–136
    See also Borrowed funds
  equity, *see* Equity funds
  nonequity, *see* Nonequity funds
  rate paid for, 47
  ratio of nonequity to equity funds,
    48–49
  source of, 43–44, 47–48

Garnishments, 139
Georgia, 101, 107, 108–109, 110, 113,
  118–119
  rate of charge, 107, 110
Goudzwaard, Maurice B., 144n
Gross income ratios, 98–102, 155

association between selected ratios
  and, 102
bad-debt ratio and, 99–100
four largest companies and all companies, 115–116
loan ceilings and, 100–101
per $100 of average loans outstand-
  ing and per loan account, 98–
  102
in thirty states, 92–102
Gross national product, compared to
  consumer credit outstanding, 4

Holders-in-due-course concept, 139
Household Finance Corporation, 8n,
  90, 114
Howard, Bion B., 135n
Hubacheck, F. B., 106n

Illegal lenders, 137, 145, 154, 155, 161
  effect of rate ceilings, 145–146, 152,
    161
  See also Loan sharks
Illinois, 100, 108–109, 111, 118–119
Income
  comparison of companies with high-
    est and lowest charges to con-
    sumers, 50–52
  disposable personal, compared to
    amount of consumer credit, 4
  "forbearance" charges, 140
  gradual decline in, 30, 31
  gross, 89, 91, 96, 144
    average loan size and, 69–71
    on consumer receivables, 31–36
    effect of company characteristics
     on, 56
    factors affecting, 56
    operating-profit relationships, 68–
     69
    portfolio risk and, 75
    ratios, *see* Gross income ratios
    trends in, 30, 31, 85
  from insurance operations, 30, 146
  from nonlending activities, 17, 30,
    42–43, 52, 146
  net-operating, 17, 42, 52–53, 90, 96–
    97
  ratios, 45, 92–97, 100–105, 142
  from personal loans, 35–36
  return on consumer receivables, 31–
    36, 42
  return on total assets, 45–47

Income tax payments, 41, 45, 62–63, 91n
  provisions for, 49–50
  trends, 38, 41
Indiana, 101, 108–109, 111, 118–119
Industrial banks, *see* Commercial banks
Insurance operations, 16, 30, 139, 146, 152
  income from, 43, 52
  regulation of, 146n, 152
Interest rates, 30, 62
  effect on profits, 49
  prime bank rate and commercial paper rate, 131–133
  trends, 47–49
Investigations, costs of, 22, 62, 150
Iowa, 100, 108–109, 111, 118–119

Kansas, 101, 108–109, 113, 118–119
Kentucky, 100, 108–109, 111, 118–119

Laws and regulations, *see* State legislation
Leverage, financial, 30, 49, 53, 143n
  effect of borrowing costs, 121, 122, 133–134
Liabilities, composition of, 125–133
  long-term financing, 126–130
  short-term financing, 125, 130–133
Licenses for offices, 89, 112
  freedom of entry and, 156–160
  requirements, 89, 156, 160n
Loan mix
  definition, 60
  operating-cost ratios and, 67–68, 79–80
  operating-profit ratios, 79–80
Loan risk
  definition, 60
  operating-cost ratios and, 66–67
  operating-profit ratios, 74–79
  See also Risks
Loan services, *see* Services, loan
Loan sharks, 12–13, 14, 19, 94, 145, 146n
  state legislation, 12–13, 160n
Loan size, *see* Size of loan
Loans
  average loans outstanding, 90, 93, 118–119
  average number of loans, 90, 118–119
  average size of loans, 90, 93, 97, 100–101, 108–109
  ceilings on, 153–156

differences in rate ceilings and, 93–94, 97
  and gross income ratio, 102
  operating ratios, 100, 103–104
  ranking by states, 108–109
  trends in, 154–156
costs per loan, 20
"higher-risk," 15–16, 18, 23
multiple, 154
number per office; *see* Number of loans per office
outstanding, 61n, 90, 108–111, 118–119
salary, 12n
size of, *see* Size of loans
Losses and charge-offs, 21, 22–24
  actual, 39
  reserves for, 24, 30
  See also Provisions for losses

Maine, 101, 108–109, 113, 118–119
Manufacturing companies, profit ratios, 19, 142
Market for small loans
  effect of finance charges on, 152
  effect of rate ceilings on, 144–145
  operating income and cost ratios, 97–98
Maryland, 94, 95, 98n, 100, 108–109, 110, 118–119, 147
Massachusetts, 101, 108–109, 111, 113, 118–119, 143
Michigan, 98n, 101, 108–109, 113, 118–119
Minnesota, 100, 108–109, 111, 118–119
Missouri, 98n
Morris Plan Banks, 137
Mortgages, 12n
  refinancing, 6n
Mutual savings banks, 2n, 16

National Association of Insurance Commissioners, 146n
National Conference of Commissioners on Uniform State Laws, 138, 154
National Consumer Finance Association, 16, 17n, 18n, 35
  analysis of questionnaires, 59–61
National Federation of Remedial Loan Associations, 13
National Foundation for Consumer Credit, 26n, 27
National Industrial Conference Board, 6

Nebraska, 98n, 101, 108–109, 113, 118–119
Net operating income ratios, 45, 92–97, 100–105, 142
  four largest companies, 115–116
  and loan ceilings, 100–101
  ratio to total assets, 45–46
  in thirty states, 92–93, 95–96, 100–102, 104–105
Nevada, 101, 108–109, 113, 118–119
New Hampshire, 91n, 97, 101, 107n, 108–109, 113, 118–119
New Jersey, 97, 98n, 100, 108–109, 111, 113, 153
New Mexico, 101, 108–109, 113, 118–119
New York, 96, 98, 100, 108–109, 111, 113, 118–119
Nine major consumer finance companies, trends in financial position, 29–53
Nonequity funds, 38, 44
  cost of, 41, 47–49
  net return on, 48–49
  ratio to equity funds, 48–49
Nonlending activities, 16, 41–43, 62, 67–68
  income from, 30, 42–43, 52, 146n
  trends in, 41–43
Nonoperating costs, 20, 38, 41
  trends, 38, 41
North Dakota, 91n, 101, 108–109, 111, 113
Note shavers, 11n
Nugent, Rolf, 11n, 12n, 13n, 146n
Number of loans per office, 20, 90, 118–119, 146
  definition, 56
  factors responsible for increasing, 88, 156
  and gross income ratio, 102
  net operating income and, 104
  operating-expense ratios and, 103
  operating-profit ratios and, 80–82, 86
  revenues per loans and, 104, 158–159
  state regulations, 88, 156
  trends, 85–86

Occupancy costs, 37–38, 40, 51, 148
  finance charges and, 52
  profit rates and, 53
Offices, loan, 20
  convenience and advantage clauses, 88n, 89, 156–160

costs and loans per office, 58
costs and revenues, 58, 159
license requirements, 89
limitations on number of, 138
number of loans per office, see Number of loans per office
utilization, 37–38, 40, 51, 96
  effect on profits, 56–57
Ohio, 101, 108–109, 113, 118–119
Operating-cost ratios, 38, 62, 102–104
  association between selected ratios and, 103
  average loan size, 63–66
  four largest companies and all companies, 115–116
  loan ceilings and, 100–101
  loan mix, 67–68
  loan risk, 66–67
  loan size, 63–66
  net operating income ratios and, 37, 104
  per $100 of average loans outstanding and per loan account, 102–104
  regulated small-loan markets, 97–98
Operating costs, 36–41, 90–91, 139
  bad-debt ratio, 91, 92
  components of, 38, 60
  direct, 149–150
    average unit cost curves, 157–158
  effect of convenience and advantage clauses, 157
  effect of risk management on, 23
  effect on rate ceilings, 143–144
  factors affecting, 37, 61–63
  finance charges and, 51–52
  nine-company averages, 36–41
  number of accounts and, 37
  occupancy costs, 37, 40
  size of loan and, 55–57, 62, 148–151
  state legislation, 88, 100–104, 149–150
  trends, 30, 31, 33, 36–41, 85
  wages and prices, 37
Operating-profit ratios
  average loan size and, 70–74
  effect of state regulations, 88
  loan mix and, 79–80
  loan risk and, 74–79
  number of loans per office and, 80–82, 86
Operating ratios
  regulated small-loan markets, 97–98
  in thirty states, 92–97, 100–101
Oregon, 101, 108–109, 111, 118–119

Overextension of consumer credit, 25–27, 152–154
Pawnbrokers, 11n
Pennsylvania, 100, 111, 154
Per-capita income ratio, 118–119
  and gross income ratio, 102
  net-operating income and, 104
  operating expense ratios and, 103
Per-capita loans outstanding, 88n, 90, 106–111, 118
  ranking of states, 108–109, 113
Personal cash loans, 1, 7, 16–17
  amount held by consumer finance companies, 11, 16–17
  competition for, 15
  development of, 11–13
  distribution by holder of, 7, 8, 10–11
  income from, 35–36
  rates, 36
  trends, 35–36
Population per loan ratios, 88n, 90, 106–111, 118–119
  effect on loan services, 88n
  ranking of states, 108–109, 113
Profits, 19, 49–50
  before taxes, 49
  comparison of companies with highest and lowest, 52–53
  consumer finance companies, 19, 52–53
  effect of financing on, 47–49
  effect of loan mix, 56, 79–80
  effect of loan risk, 56, 74–79
  effect of rate ceilings, 142–143
  effect of size of loans on, 56, 71–74
  gross income and operating-profit relationships, 68–69
  from nonlending activities, 30, 42–43, 52, 146n
  number of loans per office and, 56, 80–82
  operating-profit ratios, *see* Operating-profit ratios
  rates of, 50
  ratio of net profits to equity funds, 30, 142
  return on invested assets, 30
  role of nonequity funds, 48
  trends, 49–50
Promissory note, loans on, 12n
Provisions for losses, 24, 30, 39, 40, 51–53
  high-charge companies, 51–52
  increases in, 38, 39

profit rates and, 53
state legislation, 88
trends, 38–40

Rate ceilings, 87, 151–152
  augmented, 147, 161
  differences in loan ceilings and, 93–94, 97–98
  difficulty in legislating, 99, 151–152
  effect on higher risks, 144–145
  effect on consumers, 142–145
  effect on illegal lenders, 145–146, 152, 161
  effect on profits, 143–144, 161
  effect on services, 143–144, 146
  graduated rates, 94n, 97–98
  level of, 142–147
  need for, 156
  related to size of loans, 147–148
  relationship to finance charges, 138, 139–153
  setting, 144–145, 161
  on size of credit extensions, 153
  slope of, 97, 147–151, 161
  state regulation, 93–95, 161
Rates, 97
  fees in addition to, 107
  regulated small-loan markets, 97
  state regulation, 93–95
  system of disclosing charges, 107n
Refinancing, charges for, 152
Remedial loan societies, 12n, 13, 137
Renewals, servicing costs, 150
Repair and modernization loans, 1, 7
Resources, effective use of total, 30, 43–44
Restraint on entry, 103–104, 112, 156–160
  ranking of states, 113
  state regulations, 88–89
Retained earnings, 38
Returns
  on consumer receivables, 31, 45–46
  on total assets, 45–47
Risk-bearing base, 122, 128
Risks
  effect on costs, 56
  increase in higher-risk loans, 30
  management policies, 22–24, 90, 139–140
    effect of credit standards on, 22–24
    effect of rate ceilings on, 144–145
  need for counseling services, 25–27
  operating-cost ratios and, 66–67

operating-profit ratios and, 19, 74–79
social implications of, 22–24
Robinson, L. N., 12n, 13n
Royal Commission on Banking and Finance, 151
Russell Sage Foundation, 12–13, 14n

Salary costs, 37–38, 40, 62, 148
finance charges and, 52
profit rates and, 53
Salary loans, 12n
Sales finance companies, 2, 137, 139
automobile paper, 14
cash-lending subsidiaries, 2, 7n, 11
competition and diversification, 15–16
consumer instalment credit held by, 7–11
cost of borrowing, 122, 134
finance charges, 20
functions, 13–14
losses, 24
personal cash loans, 7, 8, 10
senior debt ratio, 134
wholesale paper, 134
Sales finance credit, 35–36, 55, 95
operating-cost ratios, 69
operating-profit ratios, 77–80
Savings and loan associations, 2n, 16
Seaboard Finance Corporation, 90, 114
Selden, Richard T., 130
Services, loan
convenience and advantage clauses, 112–114
effect of other loan laws, 111–112
effect of rate ceilings on, 143–144, 146
effect of state regulations on, 87–89, 105–114
effect on costs, 18–21, 62, 95
laws and regulations, 15
ranking of states, 105–112
Siegel, Sidney, 117
Simpson, William Hays, 96n
Size of loans
average, 18, 35, 90, 92–93, 97, 100–101, 108–109, 115–116
ceilings on, 87–88, 95, 138, 153–156, 161
ancillary loan laws, 153–155
need for uniform legislation, 153–154
reasons for, 154, 156
commercial banks, 20
consumer finance companies, 20

effect on costs and profits, 55–57, 62
gross-income ratios and, 69–71
high-cost multiple, 154
increase in, 30, 35
operating-cost ratios and, 63–66, 148–151
operating-profit ratios and, 71–74
restrictions on, 153–156
state legislation, 15, 153–154
Smith, Paul F., 17, 19n, 20, 29n, 53n, 61n
South Carolina, 101, 107, 108–109, 110, 112n, 113, 153
State legislation, 15, 87–120, 137–162
basic data and concepts, 89–92
differences in rate and loan ceilings, 93–95
effect on market for small loans, 87–88, 97–98
effect on operating profits, 88
effect on risk, 88
effectiveness in attracting capital, 110
gross income ratios, 98–102
historical development, 12–13
limitation on number of offices, 138, 156–161
loan services, 87–89, 105–112
effect of convenience and advantage clauses, 112–114
against loan sharks, 12–13, 160n
on loan size, 15, 88, 138, 153–156
net operating income ratios, 104–105
objectives of, 17–18, 106
operating expense ratios, 98–104
operating income and cost ratios, 92–97
profitability of operations, 87
protective philosophy, 87–88, 95–96, 106, 107, 110
re-evaluation needed, 136–162
results of inadequate, 95–96
small-loan statutes, 12–13, 87–89
standard of protection, 111–112

Uniform Consumer Credit Code, 138
need for, 160
rate ceiling problem, 151–152
restrictions on debtor's and creditor's remedies, 138
Uniform Small Loan Law, 13, 137, 153, 156, 160n
background, 12–13, 137
concepts and principles, 137
protective features, 107n, 160n

Upton, R. M., 135n
Usury laws, 11, 88n, 95, 107, 137, 141

Virginia, 98n, 100, 108–109, 113, 118–119

Wage earners, need for cash loans, 11, 13

Washington, 101, 108–109, 111, 118–119
West Virginia, 91n, 96, 100, 108–109, 111, 118–119
Wholesale financing, 16
Wisconsin, 94, 95, 98n, 100, 108–109, 111, 112